# CENTRAL CITY

## AND

# BLACK HAWK

### Colorado

# Then

## and.

# Now

## Frank R. Hollenback

SAGE BOOKS

Denver

Sage Books are published by

Alan Swallow, 2679 So. York St., Denver 10, Colo.

# CENTRAL CITY

# AND BLACK HAWK

# THEN AND NOW

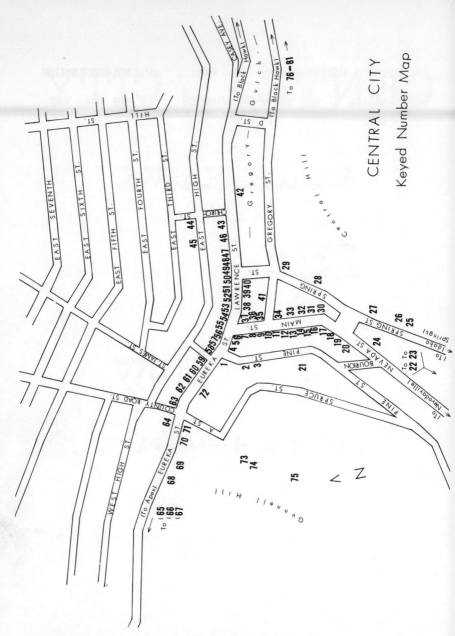

CENTRAL CITY
Keyed Number Map

**NUMBER KEY:** The numbers on this map refer to buildings; these are the same numbers as those found in the text describing each building and as those found under the pictures showing the buildings.

# FOREWORD

This book is dedicated to the thousands of visitors who walk the streets of Central City and Black Hawk each year wondering about the buildings and other man-made structures: Who built them, when, why, and what 's the story behind each one?

In scope, this is concerned with commercial buildings, or "blocks" as they were called, churches, schools, town and county offices, monuments, and a few mine structures and dwellings. (The residences of Central City and Black Hawk would fill another book but these, with one or two exceptions, are not discussed here.)

This treats of an old train now on display, for example, if that can be called a monument, and the old roadbed over which the train ran because that is also a memento of the past.

It was first intended that only those man-made features which are still very much in evidence be described, but here again are several exceptions: The Hooper brickyard has vanished without leaving a trace, but it is worthy of discussion because most of the brick used in rebuilding Central City after the big fire in 1874 came from this plant. The parking lot with a past, at the junction of Spring and Nevada Streets, the Glory Hole, and the Face on the Bar Room Floor, are a few other exceptions, because they are star attractions in this era of Central City.

In Black Hawk, behind the motel, once stood the Fifty Gold Mines mill and before that, on the same site, was the first quartz mill set up in Colorado, the Black Hawk mill that gave the town its name.

Time-wise, everything is reckoned from the discovery of gold by John H. Gregory in 1859, and the gold rush that followed. The fire in 1874 destroyed most of the Central City business district. Nearly all of the present buildings were erected in 1874 or 1875, a few in the early 1880's, one in 1897, and the last large structure, the court house, was finished in 1900. After the fire Central City had three volunteer fire companies: Rescue Fire & Hose No. 1, Alert Fire & Hose No. 2, and Rough & Ready Hook & Ladder No. 1.

Black Hawk didn't have a fire; it does have some 1860-vintage buildings intact and in use. Originally, a solid strip of dwellings, stores, and mine structures extended from Black Hawk to Central City, including Mountain City which lay between. Above Central City the towns of Nevadaville and Russell Gulch once thrived. Some thought was given to describing the buildings in these two communities, but there isn't much left standing there to discuss.

Here is a rule of thumb that should prove interesting and helpful in approximating the ages of the masonry buildings. Bill Russell came up with this device. Buildings or blocks erected in the 1860's, or before the fire, have window casings with half-moon or 180 degree arches. Those built since the fire, and for several decades thereafter, have flatter arches, while those erected in the 1890's and later have the contemporary rectangular casings. To illustrate: Note the half-circle windows of the Register block, built in 1862; the flatter-arch casings of the upper Harris block, an 1874 building; and the rectangular windows of the 1897 Parteli block. There are exceptions, of course, where forms of one era overlap into the next.

The mortar-less stone retaining walls, particularly noticeable in Gregory Gulch between Black Hawk and Central City, deserve special attention. The skill employed in erecting these masonry wonders is often credited to the Cornishmen who came to work in the mines. Others say it is the craftsmanship of southern Europeans, also attracted to the mines in the early days. Actually, the practice was probably born of necessity at a time when all space in the gulches and hillsides was used and mortar was scarce. The stone arch at the Bobtail tunnel portal is an example of this art at its best.

More than one hundred man-made landmarks of Central City and Black Hawk are traced, each numbered and keyed against numbered photos and corresponding numbers on the Central City map. The text and photos establish the link between "then" and "now," both in Central City and in Black Hawk. The style "Schonecker & Mack," for example, is used because it was the advertised name, not "Schonecker and Mack." Where possible to do so, the name of the orginal owner or builder, or a name established by the newspaper of the day, is used to identify a building. Where even these are not available, the name of a one-time occupant is applied.

Central City's economic life, and the history of its commercial buildings, can be divided into four phases (the same thing is largely true of Black Hawk). The first period concerns buildings erected in the 1860's, or before the fire; the second, those put up after the fire; the third, the buildings vacated and empty during the decline of mining; and last, the renaissance period from the late 1920's to the present.

This deals primarily with buildings that survived the fire, the ones built afterward, and the earlier occupants of those in each category.

Nothing can be said of the long periods during which many buildings were vacant, nor is it feasible to attempt a description of the ebb and flow of present-day tenancy.

Central City after the great fire. In the foreground, walls of the express office stand intact. In the ruins beyond, looking up Main Street, the Roworth block and the shells of several others are seen, while at the far end of Main the Seavy building, presently occupied by the Mining and Historical Museum, is unscathed but not unscared. (Note reddened walls when viewing structure close-up.) Spring Street winds down hill in background. *Denver Public Library Western Collection.*

# CONTENTS

Note to the reader: Throughout the book buildings are
keyed by number. This number appears on the frontis-
piece map, at the heading of discussion of each building,
and under the picture of each building.

# CENTRAL CITY

Gold was discovered in the gulch that now bears his name by John H. Gregory, a Georgian, in the spring of 1859. By the following summer, Gregory Gulch, from the site of what is now Black Hawk on North Clear Creek, to the junction of Eureka, Nevada, and Spring Gulches one mile above, swarmed with gold hunters. The gulches were crowded with tents, shanties, sluice boxes, and the good and bad of humanity.

In May of 1859, William N. Byers, founder of the *Rocky Mountain News* in Denver, had pitched his tent at the head of Gregory Gulch near what is now the corner of Main and Lawrence streets, and had suggested a name for the camp. At about the same time, Hugh A. Campbell had opened a supply store and hung out the sign, Central City. Near the end of the summer in 1860 Nathaniel Albertson, John Armour, and Harrison G. Otis platted the townsite of Central City, "its site being nearly central between the locality of the Gregory Diggings and that of the upper mines of Nevada Gulch." There may be other versions of this early history.

By the end of 1860, Central City had attained great importance as the mining and supply center for the surrounding districts. An estimated 6,000 persons were in the area. It became the county seat when Gilpin County was organized in the winter of 1861-62, and was incorporated by an act of the territorial legislature March 11, 1864.

Central City and Gilpin County grew and prospered, although many disappointed gold seekers returned to their homes in "the states." Mining suffered a set-back due to technical difficulties in the mid-60's, but the trouble was remedied by perfection of N. P. Hill's matting furnace or smelter in 1867 in Black Hawk.

Shortly after 10 A.M. on the morning of May 21, 1874, fire broke out in a shanty occupied by Chinese laundrymen in Dostal alley near Spring Street. The flames spread slowly at first, although there was neither an official fire-fighting organization nor water to stop the fire. So after consuming the frame shanties, the flames spread to Main Street and down both sides to Lawrence, and to Eureka, where the fire was finally stopped by the Register building on one side of the street, and the Teller House on the other. On Main Street, the fireproof Roworth block escaped.

Central City in 1875, or late 1874, after reconstruction. *Denver Public Library Western Collection.*

On Lawrence, the Raynolds building, or perhaps the Freas building, blocked the fire. Up on Spring Street the fireproof Seavy building was spared.

Word of the fire reached Golden by telegraph. The Colorado Central ran a special train loaded with a fire engine on a flat car to Black Hawk in record time. Even though the "Excelsior Boys" pulled their apparatus up the gulch to Central City in all haste, they were too late and the fire ran its course.

Fortunately, there were no fatalities although many families were homeless and merchants who could were obliged to find temporary quarters in the Raynolds or Register buildings—if they had any merchandise left to sell.

Writing about the fire years later, Frank C. Young* recalled the fateful 21st of May in 1874: "It has come at last!

"We have been predicting it, discussing it, dreading it—doing everything, in fact, but preparing for it—for lo!—these ten years.

---

*Frank C. Young, *Echoes from Arcadia,* 1903.

"Today the town has been laid low by fire; and tonight a thousand luckless people—half-crazed men, hysterical women, and whimpering little ones—are camped on the mountainside, under the open sky, while the stars shine down upon a broad level waste of glowing cinders on the plateau below them where this morning stood their homes."

*The Daily Register* responded: "It may be truthfully affirmed that the great calamity which swept away at a breath the foundations of our city, came to us as a providential interposition, for without this mighty shock there would have been no such mighty awakening as we have witnessed.

"All that was needed was a beginning, a strong resolute leadership. A few brave men stepped to the front . . . hosts of workmen appeared on the scene as if by magic. Millions of brick ordered, forests decimated of lumber, the entire carrying capacity of railroads levied upon to supply the demand. There was a general smashing of coffins and casting off of dry bones for new ones with plenty of marrow in them. . . ."

Reconstruction began immediately—within hours, in fact—after the fire of May 21, 1874. Five days later school was resumed. The night of May 26, council met in the Raynolds Beehive to consider street widths and other problems of rebuilding. The newspaper warned that "every effort should be made to keep the discussion from becoming acrimonious."

Council decided "Eureka and Lawrence Sts., from Pine to the eastern limit should be 45 feet; Main St., 50 feet the entire length; Gregory St., 40 feet; Spring St., 40 feet; High St., 30 feet." In summary action, the body proposed "as soon as possible to provide a fire department with one or two machines of approved manufacture and water facilities for any emergency . . . insurance savings will pay for it in two years!"

On May 29—"the citizens have made up their minds to have a city second to none in Colorado." It was expected that within a short time the Central City townsite would be covered with a government patent issued by the Land Office. Council outlawed all wooden buildings except those of a very temporary nature. Sidewalk construction was progressing. Most of the ruins and debris on Main Street had been cleaned up within a short time. Permits for temporary shanties were issued, the first, the paper noted, for a saloon; the last, for a shoe repair shop. The editor remarked wryly that the permit committee seemed to have an eye on the spiritous needs of the citizens, rather than for their soles.

Early in June, residents were warned by a mayor's proclamation that the time was drawing near to get a U. S. title to their property. To do this they would have to file on their lots. There was a brisk demand for carpenters and other artisans, a situation which was to hold throughout

1874. Judge Harley B. Morse put up the first permanent building after the fire. It was a single-story brick next to the Register building; and was ready for occupancy within nine days. (The second story was added later.)

In the first week of August, business men were warned to start building at once if they had any intentions of doing so in 1874 because of the advancing season. Streets were being graded, sometimes through solid rock, thus "eliminating much profanity and broken wagon wheels." The sidewalk under construction between Central City and Black Hawk was said to be one of the most-needed improvements.

New fireproof brick blocks were coming up all over the business section, but there was some complaint over the shortage of bricklayers and carpenters. The local brick yard of Thomas Hooper supplied brick for many of the blocks under construction. (Buildings were popularly known then as "blocks," especially if there were two or more storefronts. Henceforth, the two words "block" and "building" will be used interchangeably, as they were then.)

A few contracts were held up because of slow delivery on cut stone from the valley. Some stone was quarried on upper Eureka Street. About the delays on cut stone from valley sources, the newspaper said: "At this time delays are dangerous. No one can afford to lose an hour or a day, much less a week, at this season of the year."

Alderman Collier hoped to have most of the sidewalks in place by November 1, 1874. Those on Eureka, Main and Lawrence Streets were seven and one-half feet in width. And now a continuous strip of walk stretched from Turner Hall on Gregory Street almost to the lower end of Black Hawk.

This was a transition period marked with makeshift deals: merchants scrambling into the few unscathed buildings, some doubling up with others, or hurrying to secure space in the newly-finished blocks. The most active builders and contractors were Mansel H. Root and Mullen & McFarlane who totalled over $100,000 in building construction in 1874. Better late than never, the city fathers advertised for bids on a water works pipeline for domestic and fire protection purposes.

The building boom continued into 1875 with an estimated $175,000 worth of construction recorded for the year. Chief among the new "bricks" were the Hanington & Mellor, the Mellor & McFarlane, and Hense's new block on Main Street.

Colorado became the thirty-eighth state upon admission to the Union July 4, 1876. Fourteen days later the following news was published in

12

Central City about 1881. Railroad reached city in 1878 but tracks are not visible in photo. Temple of Fashion building was razed later. The new roof trusses had not been placed atop Armory Hall. *Denver Public Library Western Collection.*

Central City: "Prepare yourselves, lot owners, to provide yourselves with deed thereto, direct from the mayor." This meant that a United States land patent had been issued in trust for the owners of Central City property by the commissioner of the General Land Office on December 23, 1875. An attached proviso stated that no title should subsequently be acquired "to any mine of gold, silver, cinnabar or copper, or to any valid mining claim or possession under existing laws." In other words, deeds could not be issued to cover mining claims, or to supersede existing mining claims.

After the United States patent was issued for the Central City townsite, owners of town lots received what was known as a mayor's deed to their property. A very large number of Central City property titles are based upon deeds issued by Mayor B. W. Wisebart in 1876.

Years later, writing about people of Central City in the post-fire period, Frank Young reminisced: "Its traders, Jew and Gentile, while enterprising and aggressive, are in the main men of character and often of high respectability and many of them, as time passes, hold prominent places in public councils, city and territorial.

13

"The greater part of its population is native American. There is a fair sprinkling of quiet and thrifty Germans, several hundred Celts, and some few Scandinavians. In the last two or three years there has been a steady influx of robust, stout-chested, pink-cheeked lads from the tin mines of Cornwall, and these promise in time to outnumber all but the native element." Lastly, he was talking about the Cousin Jacks (and their Tommy-Knockers) from Wales.

(Frank C. Young was cashier at the First National Bank of Central City. He had come out from New York in 1865 at the age of 21, and for a spell tried his hand at placer mining. After a stint of Gilpin County journalism, he became associated with Warren Hussey's bank and later, at the First National Bank, saved securities and other valuable papers during the fire. He was a moving spirit behind the Gilpin County Opera Association.)

Frank Young explained about the name Little Kingdom of Gilpin: "It is largely because of its recognized activity and prominence in affairs that for years have been steadily leading up to this great culmination, that the district is this year [1876] christened the 'Little Kingdom of Gilpin.'"

In Frank C. Young's book, one chapter is titled: The End of the Cycle. Under it, he wrote: "It is with no little hesitating that I write the above title to what must be the final chapter . . . for I cannot help feeling that in doing so I run the risk of being misunderstood by many good people . . . who will continue to call Central City their home long after this year of 1880, which I have set as the closing one of the 15 that are here assumed as constituting the 'golden age' of the mountain colony. But it must be apparent that the process of disintegration is under way. . ."

This "process of disintegration" could be accounted for in two ways: First, the apex of Gilpin County's mineral production was reached in 1871, whereas over in Lake County, around Leadville, production reached a peak in 1882, jumping $9 million between 1878 and 1879. The shift was to Lake County, although Gilpin County in 1880 still had many fruitful years ahead—but the trend was down.

Another explanation of the so-called "process of disintegration" lay in the fact that by 1880 many Central City residents, having made their stake by then, found they could live in Denver and manage their mining or business interests from there. In any event, there was a great exodus to the "Queen City" which may have caused a disintegration in Central City society life, anyway.

In 1880, there was no effective central system to supply domestic water.

The switchback or highline between Central City and Black Hawk shortly after completion in 1878. *Charles Weitfle photo. Denver Public Library Western Collection.*

Central City around 1900. Note passenger train arriving, ball park, and completed Catholic Church. *Denver Public Library Western Collection.*

Even the few wells became dry as the mines went deeper and caused a lowering of the water table as they were pumped out. Drinking water sold on the streets of Central City at 25c a bucket. (At the same time Leadville reported "water had been reduced to 40c a barrel and will soon be cheap enough to drink.")

Gilpin County led the state in gold production from 1859 to 1893 (when Cripple Creek came on the scene). Up to that time, 15 mines in the county had each produced more than $5 million, and 15 others accounted for more than $1 million each.

Mines and independent miners turned their gold into one of the three banks in Central City. It was usually in the form of a retort, which was the residue left after the amalgam of gold and mercury was distilled, the mercury driven off as vapor (and condensed to be used again), leaving the gold retort. Each day the newspaper carried reports of gold retorts sold to the various banks. For example, on April 3, 1880: "William Fullerton left with the First National Bank a retort of 502 ounces for over $8,000."

16

Gilpin County's maximum mineral production occurred in 1871 when $3,359,240 worth of gold, silver and copper were mined.* Although lead and zinc occur in the ore deposits of the county, it wasn't until 1873 that records were kept for lead, and 1904 for zinc. There are some pitchblend deposits in the county.

The decline in mining began in 1897, and has continued downward ever since. There was some gold mining revival during the depression but whatever gains were made ceased upon the country's entry into war in 1941, and the government ukase that halted all gold mining as nonessential. After the war, labor and equipment costs were too high for gold mines to operate profitably against a price of $35 per ounce.

Should this reference to gold retorts be confusing, bear in mind that the gold produced in mills (from extractive hydrometallurgy) was usually in retort form, while the gold produced in smelters (from extractive pyrometallurgy) was usually in bar, ingot, or—well, gold brick form.

## Mayors of Central City

| | |
|---|---|
| 1865 - 1866 | Joseph W. Watson |
| 1866 - 1867 | William M. Slaughter |
| 1867 - 1868 | Robert Teats |
| 1868 - 1871 | William Roworth    (Merchant) |
| 1871 - 1872 | Hugh Butler    (Lawyer) |
| 1872 - 1874 | Thomas Mullen    (Builder and contractor) |
| 1874 - 1876 | H. Jacob Kruse    (Merchant) |
| 1876 - 1877 | B. W. Wisebart    (Merchant) |
| 1877 - 1878 | George E. Randolph    (Mining) |
| 1878 - 1879 | Peter McFarlane    (Builder and contractor) |
| 1879 - 1880 | Thomas I. Richman    (Mining) |
| 1880 - 1881 | John Best    (Druggist) |
| 1881 - 1882 | John Best and Peter McFarlane |
| 1882 - 1884 | H. M. Hale    (Educator) |
| 1884 - 1886 | Alvin Marsh    (Lawyer) |
| 1886 - 1887 | R. B. Williams    (Livery owner) |
| 1887 - 1888 | Bartholomew Robins |
| 1888 - 1889 | Frederick Kruse    (Merchant, industrialist) |
| 1889 - 1890 | Samual V. Newell    (Merchant) |
| 1890 - 1891 | John Truan    (Engineer) |
| 1891 - 1892 | S. I. Lorah    (Mining) |

*Charles W. Henderson, *Mining in Colorado*, 1926.

| | | |
|---|---|---|
| 1892 - 1893 | Ferdinand French | |
| 1893 - 1894 | J. C. McShane | (Merchant) |
| 1894 - 1895 | R. A. Campbell | (Banker) |
| 1895 - 1896 | R. B. Williams | (Livery owner) |
| 1896 - 1900 | John C. Jenkins, Sr. | (Hardware merchant) |
| 1900 - 1903 | B. E. Seymour | (Dry Goods merchant) |
| 1903 - 1904 | Fredrick Kruse | (Merchant, industrialist) |
| 1904 - 1908 | Ll. P. Davies | (Druggist) |
| 1908 - 1910 | W. O. Jenkins | (Banker) |
| 1910 - 1913 | Thomas Cody | (Coal dealer) |
| 1914 - 1919 | Robert Wilkinson | (Mining) |
| 1920 - 1921 | W. J. Stull | (Publisher) |
| 1922 - 1924 | Charles A. Frost | (Mining) |
| 1925 - 1927 | H. H. Lake | (Banker) |
| 1928 - 1933 | Robert Wilkenson | (Mining) |
| 1934 - 1936 | Earl Quiller | (Merchant) |
| 1937 - 1940 | C. O. Richards | (Mining) |

Nearly all of the business and professional men of Central City participated in mining activities, not only as purveyors of goods and services, but also as investors and mine owners. Most were speculators, or they wouldn't have left the states in the first place. Nearly without exception, while they may have begun life in Central City as, say, merchants, it wasn't long before mining shared a part or all of their attention. And the same thing goes for the doctors and lawyers.

There were numerous exceptions, of course, and needless to say not all who went into mining ventures retired to Grant Avenue in Denver. Many did migrate to that or other rich strips in Denver, but continued to look after mining and business interests in Central City and Gilpin County.

Frank Hall* wrote of Gilpin County: "The record of its vanished years is replete with glorified triumphs, the sudden accumulation of fortunes, the splendid social amenities, shadowed at times with calamities, failures, disappointed hopes, millions recklessly squandered, tragedies and despair."

## 1. The Teller House

The Teller House, perhaps the best-known, man-made landmark of Central City, had its inception February 3, 1870, when Henry M. Teller

*Frank Hall, History of the State of Colorado, 1889-1895.

1

offered to build a $60,000 hotel provided that the citizens would take $25,000 worth of stock. Perhaps it went back even before 1870. Frank C. Young* wrote years later: "We badly needed a hotel. The main hostelry, the Conner House, cannot be said to be inviting in either its inner or outer respects. It served its purpose well enough in log cabin days. . . . There are others: Central has its St. Nicholas, and Black Hawk its St. Charles, besides several others not yet cannonized. . . ."

Frank Young continues: "It is very evident that a hotel we must have, and that conclusion is no sooner reached than the little community gathers itself to take action, for it has never been slow to take action . . . to face emergencies, and public spirit is by no means lukewarm. A prominent citizen steps to the front to undertake the execution as soon as the plan takes form; the people back him up with a subsidy, to the extent of their financial capacity; and as part of his reward, when the structure is completed, it takes his name. It is a great event . . . work is pushed night and day . . . stone by stone and brick by brick for many weeks. . . .

"From the aesthetic point of view, one may say (with deference to the architect, who, I believe, is still within shooting distance at the time of this writing) that the hotel is not a masterpiece of construction. Judged by its exterior it might easily be taken for a New England factory, and cut off a story or two and it might pass fairly well for a cavalry barracks."

The Teller House was erected by Milton D. Owen who is also credited with construction of the Episcopal Church and the high school building in Central City. Begun in the summer of 1871—"before winter sets in the roof is on the building"—it was finished and occupied by July 1872. Young continued: "Another summer has begun before the interior receives its finishing touches and we can announce to the world that we can feed and house them as well as take them in as business partners if so disposed."

The grand opening ball on June 27, 1872, was a gala event. Nearly 200 of the faithful turned out in addition to the visitors from neighboring towns. The *Register* with justifiable pride pointed out that the Teller House was the largest hotel in Colorado, Denver excepted. It was described as five stories high (including the basement) and had 150 rooms, a laundry, shops, and cost $110,000. The barber shop of Jones & Urick (three chairs, the largest and best in the country—hot and cold showers, 50c, day or night) did business in the basement. William H. Bush opened

---

*Frank C. Young, *Echoes from Arcadia*, 1903.

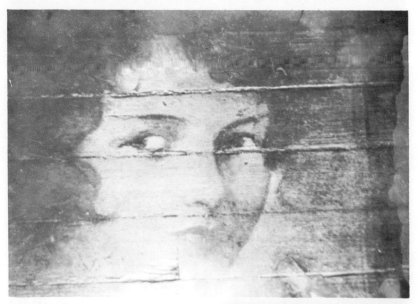

The Face on the Bar Room Floor
at the Teller House.

Billy Hamilton, for many years
keeper of the keys to the Opera
House, dusting off the Face on the
Bar Room Floor. *Claude Powe
Collection.*

the hotel and remained seven years as manager before going to the
Windsor in Denver, and the Clarendon in Leadville.

Later, in 1874 after the fire, the Rocky Mountain National Bank occupied the corner on the ground floor at Pine and Eureka Streets, remaining
there until the bank was closed late in 1915. (In January, 1916, it was
reported that fixtures of the Rocky Mountain Bank "have been stored in
the basement of the Teller House. Counters will remain for several tenants who already have taken offices in the room.")

21

Ed H. Lindsey's "The Elevator" was the drinking place in the hotel. Other businesses came, tarried and flourished or failed in the Teller House over the years.

On the occasion of President Grant's visit to Central City April 29, 1873, a path of silver bricks was laid to the door of the Teller House for him to trod. (Since Gilpin County was first and foremost a gold producing camp, the silver ingots were imported from the Caribou silver mines of nearby Boulder County.)

William Aitcheson, jewelry manufacturer, together with Lazaras, Morris & Co., spectacles and eyeglasses, occupied another ground floor suite at the Teller House in 1874 before moving into the Register building across the street.

For years after the opening, the Teller House guest register was filled with the names of actors, artists, industrialists, engineers, authors, clerics, tourists, and probably a goodly number of con men. Number one signer was the architect.

The *Register* on February 3, 1875, noted that "for the past few days painters have been working at the Teller House. Brother Bush means to be clean, even if he is not pretty." The next bit of modernizing came in June of that year, a forerunner of the electronic age, perhaps, when it was announced that "by tomorrow night the electrical annunciator in the Teller House will be ready for business."

Many owners and managers came and went at the Teller House: Bush, Breese, Sherick, Wentworth, Grace Brooks, to name a few, but with the decline in mining there came a decline in Teller House activity and revenue.

The renaissance, of course, changed all that and more. Nowadays, seemingly, one of the main attractions is The Face on the Barroom Floor at the Teller House. It's fame, apparently, has spread to the ends of the earth. Herndon Davis, staff artist on *The Denver Post*, painted the face in the summer of 1936 as a bit of high-jinx one night while staying at the hotel. The idea originated with Hugh d'Arcy's ballad "The Face on the Bar Room Floor."

Face on the Bar Room Floor

'Twas a balmy summer evening and a goodly crowd was there,
   Which well nigh filled Joe's barroom on the corner of the square,
   As song and witty sayings came through the open door,
   A vagabond crept slowly in, and posed upon the floor.

22

"Give me a drink,—that's what I want,—I'm out of funds you know,
  When I had cash to treat the crowd, this hand was never slow.
  You laugh as though this pocket had never held a sou;
  I once was fixed as well, my boys, as any of you."

"I was a painter—not one that daubed on bricks and wood,
  But an artist, and for my age, was rated pretty good.
  And then I met a woman,—now comes the funny part,
  With eyes that petrified my brain and sank into my heart."

"I was working on a portrait, one afternoon in May,
  Of a fair-haired boy, a friend of mine, who lived across the way,
  And Madeline adored it, and much to my surprise,
  Said she'd like to know the man that had such dreamy eyes."

"It took not long to know him and before the month had flown,
  My friend,—he stole my darling, and I was left alone,
  Give me that piece of chalk that marks the baseball score,
  And you'll see the lovely Madeline upon the barroom floor."

Another drink,—with chalk in hand, the vagabond began
  To sketch a face that well might buy the soul of any man.
  Then, as he placed another lock upon the shapely head,
  With fearful shriek, he leaped, and fell across the picture,—dead.

                                    —H. Antoine D'Acy

## 2. The Henderson Block

Late in October, 1879, Dave Henderson had a crew grading two lots
on Pine Street in preparation for erection of a two-story brick building
which was finished in December.

Henderson came almost directly from Scotland to Russell Gulch in 1859.
His mining and mechanical skills became legendary. While in Russell
Gulch, he located and mined placer deposits that others overlooked or
were unable to operate profitably.

In 1878, Henderson joined John Jenkins and Dan McKay to buy out
the hardware firm of Ladd & Schuyler on Lawrence Street. Henderson, in
the role of inventor and craftsman, built and operated a screen perforating
machine (on display at the museum), as well as other mechanical devices,
in the tin and iron shop of the hardware store. He also won fame as a
master gunsmith.

The brick building on Pine Street was best known for many years as
the office and residence of Drs. Asquith and Ashbaugh, brothers-in-law
and Central City physicians.

Dave Henderson died in 1909, leaving an estate estimated to be over
$100,000. The story is told that after his demise tin cans stuffed with
twenty dollar gold pieces were found in the walls of the building.

23

21

3                                                    2

### 3. The Richville House

This frame house, although directly in the path of the flames, escaped without damage in the fire of 1874, and from this incident another legend was born. A very strange anomaly developed. Not only did this wooden structure come out of the holocaust without a scar, but it was one of the few buildings in Central City covered at all with fire insurance. So the story comes down that the owner, probably wringing his hands in anguish, watched the flames race along Pine Street, jump over his house, and cheat him out of insurance money for a newer and better home.

The house was built in 1868 or 1869 by Ann and Robert Richville on a lot deeded to them by Richards in 1866. The Richvilles sold the house in 1875 to Burrell, who may have been the druggist conducting a business for a short time in the Harris block.

In the 1930's, this was the home of Oscar Williams, a Gilpin County sheriff and livery operator, and son of colorful R. B. (Dick) Williams, Central City lawman of an earlier generation.

## 4. The Post Office

The fire of 1874 destroyed the Central City Post Office, and then most of the letters and papers which had been moved to a supposedly safe place in the Congregational Church basement.

Later in 1874, the post office was installed in the upper portion of the new First National Bank building, at the corner of Pine and Eureka Streets. Eben Smith, postmaster only a short time when the fire struck, took immediate steps to house the post office in suitable quarters in the new building.

In 1874, from both new and old locations, the post office sold $4,000 worth of stamps; received 400, and transmitted 350 letters daily. During the year, $50,000 worth of domestic money orders were issued while only $10,000 was paid out, and $10,000 in money orders was sent to England.

As soon as the building was finished, and the post office was being moved into the ground floor, new office and dwelling tenants were occupying the upstairs. For many years, the Colorado Telephone Company's switchboard and office were in these rooms.

In November 1885, Mr. Burgess, manager of the telephone company, "was fitting rooms over the post office where the main office of the telephone company was installed."

A later occupant of the post office space was Sol Bacharach. After the fire, he had also erected a building, or "block," below Hense's on Lawrence. This he vacated, occupied some space across the street, and at another time conducted business in the former post office before moving to Colorado Springs in the 1890's.

Central City's last undertaker, Ed Hamlik, occupied the premises until about 1930. His sister has been the city clerk for many years.

Note that here are four separate units in the First National Bank building complex. All have the same architectural design and features but may be identified separately by the different color each is painted.

Back to the telephone company upstairs—in 1882, the company had 33 subscribers; in 1885, 39 subscribers. In 1897, the company proudly announced that 250 calls a day were being handled at the local office.

## 5. Chase & Sears

Wedged between the First National Bank and the post office, Chase & Sears operated a tobacco and newsstand for a few months until sometime

25

6                          5        4

in 1875 when Albert Lintz bought the business. Here stood Central City's only cigar store Indian.

In September of 1885, Mark B. Hyndman, one-time owner of the City Book Store, and Evan Morgan sold cigars, tobaccos and fruit here as Morgan & Co.

## 6. The First National Bank Block

This building, or block, has an illustrious history.

Beginning early in 1863, Warren Hussey, Salt Lake banker, opened a branch of his Denver banking house in Central City. Joseph A. Thatcher was the manager. The business expanded and was sold to Thatcher, Standley & Co. in July 1870. In Central City, from this nucleus the First National Bank of Central City was organized January 1, 1874: Joseph A. Thatcher, president; Otto Sauer, Central City merchant, vice president; and Frank C. Young, rising socialite and civic leader, cashier.

Before the fire, the bank was housed at the site of the Mellor block. When the fire struck on May 21, 1874, nothing more than the frame building was destroyed. A heavy fireproof vault protected important

26

papers. Business of the bank was conducted immediately after the fire at the J. O. Raynolds' Beehive on Lawrence Street. (Here the bank shared space with several other businesses.)

Early in July 1874, the contract was let for a new building: "A large, fine, two otory, 70 feet on Eureka, 45 feet on Pine and 34 feet on Main Street. The first floor is occupied by the bank and is lighted by three large windows of French plate glass. The circular counter is of the finest walnut, the center panels of veneered French walnut. For workmanship there is nothing like it in Colorado Territory." So wrote a *Register* reporter.

A large fire and burglar-proof vault enclosing a 6,000-pound Herring safe was installed in the right hand corner of the bank. The rest of the Eureka Street front was occupied by Chase & Sears, tobacconists, and the United States Post Office.

The upper floor "accommodated one-half dozen lawyers, one physician, the clerk of the district court, and the law offices of Judge James B. Belford, Colorado's first congressman."

In the immediate area of the bank and adjacent buildings, the flume carrying Eureka creek is constructed under the bank building and street. Through the years the flume has been a problem, both in Central City and Black Hawk.

## 7. Schonecker & Mack

Louis Mack came to Central City in 1861 and opened a billiard parlor at this location. A partnership of Schonecker & Mack was formed. The fire destroyed their building, but business was resumed the very next day in a fireproof warehouse at the rear of their lot.

Like most of the other fire victims, Schonecker & Mack immediately after the fire made plans for a new building—fireproof this time, of course. In December 1874, the partners took possession of their new building adjacent to the First National Bank, on Main Street. The same architect designed both (if there was an architect) and it will be seen that the construction and style is the same, the distinguishing feature between Schonecker & Mack's and the bank building from the outside is the different color the brick is painted.

Above the billiard parlor were "five pleasant rooms, suitable for offices or sleeping quarters, three of which are rented. The building cost $3,000." So reported the *Register* in its year-end edition of 1874.

Schonecker sold out to Mack and in 1878 John Hancock purchased the building from Mack for $9,500.

Years later, Louis Mack's son erected the Mack building in Denver on the site presently occupied by the J. C. Penney store at Sixteenth and California Streets.

## 8. The Harris Block

This is the oldest of the Harris blocks on Main Street. (The third block or building is unlettered. It stands on the east side of Main at the corner of Gregory Street.)

Early in April of 1875, it was noted in the paper that "Mullen & Thomas have begun grading for the new Harris block located between Schonecker & Mack's and Van Deren's building." It was finished by July and immediately occupied by A. Rachofsky's New York Store (dry goods and clothing) which had moved up from the Roworth building.

The second floor was divided into 16 rooms, all joined by a corridor running the length of the building, access to which was gained only from stairways in the Van Deren and Schonecker & Mack buildings. No stairs were built in the Harris block.

The block was erected by Robert Harris. A word about the Harris family. Robert Harris brought his wife and children out from Plymouth, England, in the early days. They went back to England once but returned to Central City to live for a while before moving to Denver. Robert Harris died in Denver June 25, 1890 at the age of 57. One of the seven children, Ed L. Harris, was a prominent Central City figure for many years, as was his sister, Emma Harris. (See other Harris Block.)

Apparently, at first, the New York Store occupied only two-thirds of the Harris block. The druggist, H. M. Burrell, was in one of the spaces for a short time, and was succeeded there by the furniture and grocery firm of Ralph & Paynter in April 1877. Paynter had conducted a fruit store in the Granite House, while Ralph was formerly in the furniture and undertaking business on lower Lawrence Street.

Later, the New York Store for many years occupied the entire ground floor of the Harris Block.

## 9. The Van Deren Building

This was originally the Van Deren & Sauer building, Archibald Van Deren and Otto Sauer. Van Deren was one of the three original county commissioners named when Gilpin County was created by the territorial legislature in 1861. Sauer, one of the prominent merchants of the day,

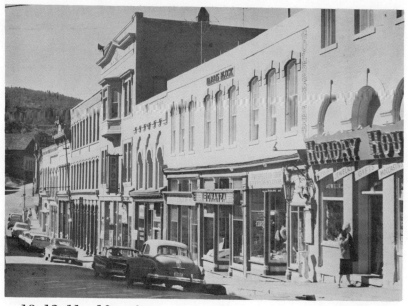

later became president of the First National Bank of Central City. Like many of his successful contemporaries, he moved to Denver and came "up from the valley" frequently to take care of his business here. Van Deren was not associated in any business in this building except in ownership of the lot upon which it stands, or so the prime deed reads.

The background is like this: In 1864, Sessler & Sauer started a business in the old Warren Hussey block at the corner of Main and Lawrence Streets, opposite the intersection. They remained a year, then sold out and went back to "the states." In the summer of 1866, they returned to Central City with a large stock of groceries and mining supplies, and opened shop at No. 2 Register building.

The firm prospered, and after two years moved to Van Deren's building on Main Street, then just completed. Came the fire in 1874 and Sessler & Sauer were burned out, along with a lot of other Main Streeters. They salvaged some stock and it was back again to No. 2 Register block.

Within three months the Van Deren building was rebuilt and away the partners went to their old location on Main Street. The firm was dissolved in October, 1874, Sessler retiring. (Somewhere along the line it has been noted that Sessler was an undertaker in Central City. It's likely that this business was conducted separately from the grocery at an establishment on Spring Street. So his ad reads, anyway.)

Sauer's grocery store in the Van Deren building, and for part of the year in the Register building, with an inventory worth $35,000 did a gross business in 1874 of $175,000. Later, Sauer moved down Main Street as will be noted elsewhere.

After the Van Deren building was refurbished, one of the upstairs rooms was occupied by Dr. W. S. Jackson, dentist. His place was described as "elegantly furnished and supplied with all of the facilities for external comfort and internal torture." L. C. Tolles, M.D., was another upstairs tenant, and the last room was occupied by Western Union.

## 10. The Mullen Building (Elks)

This was known first as "Mullen & Co's." building, built and owned by Thomas Mullen and Morris Thomas, two Central City contractors. A Mr. Beal, owner of the lot, arrived in town from the east October 1, 1874. He immediately advertised the lot for sale. Mullen lost no time in buying it (the next day, in fact), nor in starting to build (also the next day, according to accounts).

A "two-story brick," 39 by 70 feet, was finished December 15, 1874. The two street-level rental spaces were occupied immediately, one by W. F. Crawford, a druggist, the other by Weil Brothers, clothing merchants.

Crawford was described as "a genial little gentleman who had just got settled in the 'Little Drug Store' on the Miller corner when the fire hit." The following day he set up shop in the Presbyterian Church. Then he moved to a temporary shanty at his old location where he conducted business until the Mullen building was finished, after which he moved in with a $5,000 stock. Weils had a large stock of dry goods and clothing, it was reported.

Crawford didn't stay long, nor apparently did Weil. Thereafter, a meat market, photographic gallery, furniture store and other sundry enterprises were located here. Even the Misses Hamlick & Gentry, milliners and dressmakers, on April 28, 1877, moved into No. 1 Mullen block. Joseph Collier and C. Weitfle had a photographic studio here, and Will Nicholson, a meat market, after moving from the Granite House. Weitfle bought out Collier in 1878.

The Elks Club, Central City Lodge No. 557, which had been meeting at the I.O.O.F. hall since its installation by Denver Lodge No. 17 on March 23, 1900, decided in 1902 to secure club rooms of its own. On May 22, 1902, Thomas Mullen, Margaret Mullen and Morris Thomas issued a warranty deed for the two-story building to the Central City lodge. After that the Elks added a third story to the building which then became another of several in Central City to have two roofs.

## 11. The Hawley Block

This "block" is lots 10u 7 and 8 in block 1 (another kind of block) for which mayor's deeds were issued to Robert Cameron, and Hawley & Manville, respectively, after the townsite patent was issued by the United States to Central City, as trustee, for the lot owners in 1876. (Actually, practically every title in Central City originates with a mayor's deed.) Cameron and Hawley & Manville evidently decided to combine their lots and erect one large building thereon.

Taking Robert Cameron first: When the fire broke out, he was in the old Gurney building "with a stock of boots and shoes." Salvaging $2,000 worth of stock, he set up shop temporarily on the ground floor of the Baptist Church on lower Lawrence Street. Early in September of 1874, he teamed up with Henry J. Hawley and J.S.D. Manville to erect what was to be the Hawley block. Originally two stories (the third floor was added in 1875), the building cost $7,000 and was described as "one of the most cheerful in Central City."

Cameron's stock of boots and shoes was kept at a $6,500 level from which he grossed $20,000 in 1874. Mrs. Cameron's dressmaking and millinery shop occupied the second floor above the shoe store.

Hawley's involvement in the general picture is more complicated. In 1868, Hawley went into a partnership with Benjamin Lake in a grocery business Lake founded in 1862. This became the firm of Lake & Hawley and was moved to the old Van Deren building on Main Street. In 1871, J.S.D. Manville replaced Lake who then went into partnership with William Roworth in a grocery business.

The fire "cleaned out" Hawley & Manville, but before it was over they had purchased the grocery stock of Roworth & Lake whose building and establishment was the only one left standing on Main Street after the fire. It was then that the two got together with Robert Cameron to build the Hawley block.

In 1877, the Central City version of "musical chairs" got underway in earnest. Hawley bought out Manville, the firm of Roworth & Lake was dissolved. The new firm of Lake & Manville emerged and joined the gold rush to Deadwood in the Black Hills—a good example of the gold being shinier on the other side of the fence. They went into business up in Dakota Territory, but it wasn't long before that partnership was dissolved in the new Eldorado.

31

14          13   12   11

Cameron apparently didn't stay long because L. N. Schmidt opened a tailor shop there in July 1875. At another time Charles H. Berryman, "High Art" tailor occupied the space. Morrell's hardware store was also in the Cameron part, beginning Oct. 8, 1897, for some years, and in April 1906, A. Rapin moved his Mineral Palace in here from the previous location in the I.O.O.F. building.

The Hawley Merchandise Co. was incorporated in March 1880, and was destined to be in business for 56 years. Hawley died in 1923, leaving the store's affairs in the hands of Benjamin Seymour.

Seymour closed out the Hawley Merchandise Co. in 1936. On November 22, 1937, an ad appeared in the *Register-Call*: "Hawley Block for sale very cheap. See B. E. Seymour."

## 12. The I.O.O.F Building

Once known as the Teller building, Henry M. Teller's 25 by 65-foot "fireproof" was finished in September, 1874—another post-fire structure— at a cost of $6,000. One of the stores was occupied immediately by Chandler Freeman and his City Book Store; the other by Louis Schultz, shoes and boots. The upper floor was leased for one year to the I.O.O.F. lodge, just moved from Black Hawk. In 1878, the lodge purchased and renamed the building.

A word about the I.O.O.F. lodges in Gilpin County:

Rocky Mountain Lodge No. 2, chartered in Central City on June 14, 1865, was the parent lodge of the county with five charter members.

Colorado Lodge No. 3, chartered in Black Hawk May 16, 1866 with nine charter members.

Nevada Lodge No. 0, chartered in Nevadaville September 23, 1868, with six charter members.

Russell Gulch Lodge No. 46, chartered in Russell Gulch October 19, 1881 with eight charter members.

Scandia Lodge No. 60, chartered in Black Hawk July 11, 1884 with 21 charter members.

Of Chandler Freeman, it was said that "he was without peer in the book and stationery business." In March 1873, he purchased the stock of Luther Clark for $500. The next year the fire destroyed most of his stock. "Undaunted," the reporter wrote, "Freeman moved into a building next to the foundry on Eureka Street. In August 1874, he purchased the stock of Abe Search and, upon completion of the Teller building (I.O.O.F.) moved in there." By the end of 1874, Chandler had a $6,000 stock of chromos, books and stationery. Mark B. Hyndman later bought out Freeman.

Later on, W. S. Green's drug store occupied one side, and for many years A. Rapin's Mineral Palace, a jewelry store, was on the other side. Rapin moved to the Hawley block in 1906.

Rapin got a pretty bad roopin' one August day in 1910. A stranger, purporting to be a miner from Telluride, arrived in town and displayed a chunk of amalgam at various saloons. He let it be known he was short of ready cash and was ready to deal for the amalgam at an attractive price and invited any and all offers. Somehow Rapin, a jeweler experienced in buying gold amalgam, got into the act, and made the stranger an offer. The sale was conditional, depending upon the outcome of a test Rapin was to make to ascertain the purity of the gold in the amalgam. (Amalgam is a putty-like substance, a mixture of gold and mercury, an end product in the recovery of gold from gold ore.) Rapin was satisfied that the amalgam assayed high in gold and made the purchase. Paid, the seller left town immediately. Sometime later Rapin discovered that a switch had been made and his purchase was a worthless chunk of amalgamated brass shavings.

Hyndman later moved to one of the Edmundson buildings on Lawrence Street with the City Book Store, and after that went in with Evan Morgan at the post office cigar store.

14　　　　　13　　　　12

Couch's candy store, located here for many years, was a popular confectionary where reserved seat tickets for Opera House performances could be purchased. For example, when D. W. Griffith's *Birth of a Nation* came to town, tickets were sold at Couch's. Later Ed Blake operated the store.

## 13. The Roworth Building

These two buildings, while dissimilar in appearance, have always been used and sold as a unit. Built by William Roworth, or possibly Roworth brothers, these, being of brick, were the only buildings on Main Street to survive the fire in 1874. Early photos show Roworth brothers ran a bakery before 1874 in one of the buildings. But the history of each, or the two together, is obscure.

William Roworth and Benjamin Lake joined into a partnership in the 1860's with a grocery business said to have been started on a capital of $80 that grew in volume to $250,000 per year. They were credited with saving the lives of some snowbound miners in 1862, but in what way is not known.

After the fire the grocery part of the business was sold to Hawley & Manville who very shortly built and moved to a new building a few doors away on Main Street. Roworth & Lake confined their efforts to dealing in hardware, stoves, building supplies, and the manufacture of tin and copper items. They finished 1874 with a gross volume of $75,000 for the year against an inventory of $25,000, using only one of the two buildings, or sides.

When Hawley & Manville bought the grocery side the vacancy left by their departure was filled for a short time by the New York Store. Then in April 1875 it was vacant again, and an ad was printed: "For Rent— Roworth's fireproof grocery house, Main St."

In the summer of 1876, Henry Thompson moved his furniture and undertaking business into the store from Denver, and at once launched an extensive newspaper advertising program. The campaign included, among other things, the guarantee: "No more delays in undertaking. I promise to keep a full line of coffins and caskets in stock. Special attention to embalming and shipping bodies. I have a new corpse preserver. Henry Thompson, Roworth Block, Main Street, Central City." Thompson stayed a year or two and then closed out his entire business.

The firm of Roworth & Lake was dissolved May 26, 1877, and Roworth became the sole owner. Lake and J.S.D. Manville (who had also left the firm of Hawley & Manville) succumbed to the gold fever (there wasn't sufficient gold in Gilpin County) and joined the stampede to Deadwood in the Black Hills. (In Deadwood, Manville sold out to Lake in September of that year and returned to Central City sadder but wiser, he said.)

In 1882, Otto Sauer, having taken a partner, John C. McShane, vacated the Van Deren building and moved Sauer-McShane & Co. into the two old Roworth stores (see the old sign on the building front). This space was occupied for many years, first under the above style, and then as the Sauer-McShane Mercantile Co. In later times the buildings have been used as the usual shops and as a garage. In 1940, in order to make automobile storage space, the front was lowered and occupied by the Central City Motor Co.

## 14. Harris Block

This Harris block is believed to have been built in the late 70's or early 80's as a single story building.

The *Weekly Register-Call* of November 27, 1897 reported: "Miss Emma Harris has let a contract to Trebilcock & Co. for improvements in Harris' building which adjoins Sauer and McShane's grocery store. The contract calls for another floor to be added to the present building. The lower floor will contain three stores 60 feet deep." From the same paper on December 24, 1897: "J. R. Quigley & Co. are tearing down the front portion of the Harris block, and expect to have the new part finished at an early date." Apparently another contractor was called in to complete the job.

Miss Emma Harris was a daughter of Robert Harris and seemed to conduct all of the Central City business for her father. Her nephew, George D. Harris, remembers her as a remarkable woman. Ed Harris' undertaking parlors were housed for many years in the extreme left store space, while at one time the right side was tenanted by the Gilpin Dry Goods store. A. L. Davis, physician and surgeon, had offices upstairs as did A. D. Gibbs, an attorney. For a number of years the building was used as the Adler Hotel.

A word or two about Ed L. Harris. He and his sister, Emma, were two of the seven children of the Robert L. Harrises. Ed was born in Plymouth, England, December 28, 1859. After the family moved to Central City, and at the age of 20, Ed Harris got into the furniture and undertaking business with John Trezise, then in the Bacharach building on Lawrence Street.

In February 1881, Ben Wisebart, owner of the O. K. Store building on Main Street, had the building remodeled and redecorated for the tenancy of John Trezise. But in April of 1886, Ed Harris and Harry Abbott purchased the furniture stock carried by Trezise at the Bacharach building, which was separate from the undertaking business at the O. K. building on Main Street. On July 17 of that year, John Trezise sold his jewelry and undertaking business to Robert Harris. A month later Robert Harris sold the concern to his son, Ed, and Harry Abbott, who planned to run the undertaking and furniture business together—probably at the O. K. building. In September of 1886, Ed Harris went to school in Denver. By 1910, for many years established in the Harris block, Ed Harris moved to Denver and for the next 30 years was associated with I. N. Rogers & Sons. He retained the business in Central City with George Hamllick as his assistant. Harris died in Denver December 31, 1940.

All this involved detail is recounted to illustrate further how the game of musical chairs, business-wise, worked in Central City in the early days.

## 15. The Meyer Building

The two-story Meyer building was likely one of several on Main Street gutted by the fire in 1874, but rebuilt almost immediately afterward. Originally, the window casements were arched, and later modified to the present rectangular shape.

Around 1880, give or take a year or so, the Thevolie restaurant was in business here, followed by John Thezise's undertaking parlor.

In 1886, the *Gilpin County Observer* was founded in Black Hawk by a man named Crosson. After a publishing company had been formed in 1887 and Alex McLeod became editor, the paper was moved to Central City and housed in this building. Later, the *Observer* was published by Fritz Altvater and moved to the Dorris block on Gregory Street in 1897.

A saloon operated by Ignatz Meyer followed and was in business here for many years. It was probably during his tenure here that the second story was added, making it another building with two roofs.

## 16. The A.O.U.W. Building

This was known in the early days, after the fire, of course, as the O.K. building, then a one-story. Two days after the fire "rubbish was cleared away and building began," the *Register* said. The new "iron front" was finished in August at a cost of $4,000 and housed A. Jacob's O.K. store. In 1877, he sold out to the original Marx brothers.

A.O.U.W.—Ancient Order of United Workmen—Lodge No. 16 was organized in Central City February 9, 1884. In 1897, the lodge purchased the O.K. building, extended it to the rear, put on a new front, and added a second story. (Another Central City building with two roofs.)

For many years the ground floor housed the Central City post office.

21

18                    17                    16    15

74              21

19           18           17       16

At another time, a candy store was in the space. The post office was here until 1938. In it, there were said to have been separate wickets for men and women.

## 17. The Old City Hall

This is not the original name of this small, two-unit building. It is pre-1874, and more likely about 1864, in origin. A study of the walls and early photos indicates that it was gutted by the fire, with perhaps only the walls surviving, and around the shell the newer building was erected.

Old photos taken after the fire show that both the right and left sides had three arched casement windows each, such as exist now on only the left side. When the city hall was here prior to 1900, there were six high-arch window forms. In fact, still later pictures taken in the 1930's show the same thing. It wasn't until the right side was converted into a dwelling that the right front was cubed.

In the early 1870's, Tremewan's saloon was here, followed by the Arcade in the left bower. Before the city hall found a permanent home in Washington Hall it occupied the right side. (In 1900, when the court house was built, the county offices vacated Washington Hall and it was sold to Central City for a city hall.) In the 1930's, the Chain O' Mines garage took up the entire building; in later years, the right side has been a private dwelling.

## 18. Armory Hall

The Armory Hall is a Central City landmark with an unusual amount of historical meaning and interest. Up to the time of the fire in 1874, the Montana Theater on Lawrence Street together with a few deadfalls around town seemed to suffice for entertainment purposes, at least, for some forms of amusement.

The Belvidere, "a new opera house at the head of Main," was built by Henry M. Teller and Judge Silas B. Hahn and completed around August 8, 1875. It was described in the *Register* as "brick, two stories high, the second fixed for operatic affairs, with an auditorium 18 feet high, a floor 40 by 55 feet. The first floor is divided into three commodious stores lighted in front by six large windows." The original roof was flat; roof trusses were added later.

The newspaper reported on August 10, 1875, that a Steinway grand piano and elegant chairs were on the way from eastern suppliers, and that with painters finishing their work the Belvidere would be ready for the public within a few days. A few days later the paper lamented that "our new opera house is ready for dedication but we hear nothing of the dedication."

But not for long. The Belvidere was used for both amateur and professional performances. In September, 1875, the Amateur Dramatic Company advertised a "Melo-Dramatic Pantomime 'Little Red Riding Hood', followed by 'Hannah Jane' and 'Woodcocks Little Game'."

While the Belvidere may have lacked some of the Montana's glamor, it was still the hub of theatrical efforts. Another announcement followed on November 16, 1875, stating that arrangements were in progress for the grand opening of a music hall in one of the Belvidere theater rooms with Schlessinger & Lentz as impressarios.

Some doubt arose concerning the safety features of the Belvidere's upstairs floor when subjected to the weight and stress of large crowds. It came to a head on April 22, 1876 when this statement came forth: "Since the crush of last night we have been informed by the builders of the Belvidere Theater that however great the crowds there should be no apprehension for safety. McFarlane & Mullen are firm builders."

When the Amateur Dramatic Company's "The Bohemian Girl" was such a sell-out on April 17, 1877, the Belvidere's "inadequacy was realized. Consequently, an opera house was talked about and built with amazing dispatch." (Speaking of the Central City Opera House, dedicated March 4 and 5, 1878.)

Plastered across the building front in the 1880-plus period was a large sign in block letters: WESTMAN & NEWELL; then in smaller letters: HAY GRAIN FEED & COAL; and over each archway: BOARDING STABLE, and COAL OFFICE.

The Central City fire department also occupied the ground of Armory Hall for many years.

In 1886, J. S. Beaman bought this "and adjoining buildings." It was reported that he made certain improvements and for many years thereafter Armory Hall housed the Central Bottling Works, J. S. Beaman, proprietor. He lived in the adjoining building up Nevada Street. The building was also the home of the Central Athletic Club, 125 members strong. The name Armory was not used in vain, either, because around 1900, plus and minus a few years, the hall was used for various military doings of the militia or guard. For example, early in 1901 company F, First Infantry, National Guard of Colorado, held its dedication ball at Armory Hall. "It was the social event of the season . . . eighty couples . . . enjoyed themselves to the limit," the *Register-Call* society editor reported.

Speaking of society, in 1910 a fashion show was staged in Armory Hall. The building has been vacant for many years.

One of the complaints about the Belvidere concerned the poor acoustical effects in the theater. And then, too, one has only to look at the stage, even as it appears today, to appreciate the charge of "inadequacy" voiced in 1875.

Inspection of the interior reveals that, in order to improve the acoustics and provide more theater space, a partition may have been removed after the building was finished. This possibility is further borne out by the fact that the building originally had a flat roof. This was remodeled and altered by the addition of large roof trusses which may have replaced the long, longitudinal partition.

## 19. The Alhambra Theater

This building adjoining Armory Hall, while best known as the J. S. Beaman residence for many years, was at times used as the Alhambra theater. (Skeptics should consult old photos.) It may have also been one of the Shoo-Fly variety halls that abounded at various places at times around town.

The building—at least the shell—is believed to pre-date the fire of 1874, and at one time was the property of Benjamin W. Wisebart, the Central City mayor in 1876: "The east wall of the Wisebart building is the west wall of Armory Hall," the newspaper stated. It probably housed Wisebart's clothing store.

January 27, 1976, "New Company at the Alhambra," and on June 2, 1876, "the old Alhambra, idle so long, is bright tonight with a grand dance," the paper reported.

J. S. Beaman bought this building and Armory Hall in 1886, using the two as a residence and bottling works. Much earlier, there was a harness shop here.

## 20. Lampshire House

This house is herein called the Lampshire House for no other reason than it was so designated in a newspaper item in 1936. In May of that year, it was noted that W. S. Parfet had purchased from George H. Huber the brick house on Nevada Street known as the Lampshire House.

Its year of origin is about 1900. It is known to have been the residence of Mr. Bristol, a Colorado and Southern engineer; also of Peers, the postmaster in 1903; also of Walter Lampshire; and of Joseph Retallack at another time.

75

20

## 21. St. Mary's of the Assumption Catholic Church

In the spring of 1869, the Rt. Rev. John B. Lamy, Bishop of Santa Fe, was notified that the Pikes Peak region had been made a part of his diocese. (The Pikes Peak region in the 1860's included the new gold-discovered areas of what is now Colorado.) The bishop immediately dispatched the Revs. J. P. Machebeuf and J. B. Raverdy to the new country. They arrived in Denver October 29, 1860. Father Machebeuf conducted the first mass in Gregory Gulch late in that same year in the Sons of Malta Hall in Mountain City. (Other accounts say that the services were held in the Hadley building, Mountain City. Probably the lodge hall was in the Hadley building.) Mountain City was the community just below Central City. Services were conducted thereafter about once a month, depending upon the priest's visit.

The Catholics purchased a two-story frame house on Pine Street, Central City, in 1862 at the site of the present church. In September of 1863, the Rev. Thomas Smith was appointed pastor. Under his leadership the church was enlarged and plans made for a larger building. Bishop Lamy presided at the corner stone laying of St. Patrick's in 1866. Another version says that Bishop Machebeuf laid the cornerstone in 1872. The church was damaged in the fire of 1874 and for 20 years the congregation worshipped in a roofed-over basement. St. Patrick's was changed to St. Mary's of the Assumption on November 20, 1892. *The Register* adds that

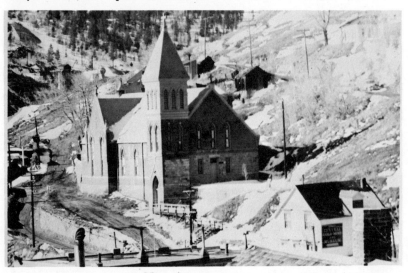

21

**22**

the present church was finished in 1893. In July 1886, Rev. J. W. Howlett preached his last sermon at St. Patrick's after a pastorate of 10 years in Central City.

## 22. Hooper's Brick Yard

Out in the vicinity of Roworth and Hooper streets once stood the Hooper brick yard. No trace of it is left. Many, if not most, of the brick buildings erected in Central City after the 1874 fire were built of Hooper brick, a sand product which would be wholly unsuited to modern construction. But it does a good job, and has for many years, provided the buildings made of it are *painted* at regular intervals. Otherwise, there is the decay and crumbling that can be seen on some structures around town.

Thomas Hooper, M.D., came to Central City with his son, Thomas, Jr., and for 18 months engaged in the drug business with J. K. Rutledge. They returned to "the states" to participate in the Civil War. After the war they came again to Central City and started brick making this time.

Seemingly, there was a demand for brick in the 60's around Central City but nothing to compare with the importance of a brickyard right after the fire.

After the senior Hooper's demise, the younger man carried on with the brick making business, not only in Central City but in Idaho Springs as well, until 1879, at least. (The 1879 directory confirms this but nothing was shown in later directories.)

In 1892, Thomas Hooper was sheriff of Gilpin County and served three terms in that office. He put in one term as treasurer of Central City and a number of years as police magistrate and justice of the peace. He died at the Soldiers and Sailors Home at Monte Vista in 1911.

Hooper brick is easily discernable in buildings around town; the Teller House is built wholly of it.

## 23. The Glory Hole

Large numbers of visitors each year drive up to see the Glory Hole but perhaps wonder just what they are looking at when they get there— besides a deep, gaping hole in the ground.

23

First of all, "glory-hole" is the term for a certain mining method. (It can be used either as a noun or as a verb: *The glory hole . . .* or *they were glory holing . . .* , and so on.)

A glory hole is simply a man-made funnel in a massive mineralized rock formation, where the rock is drilled and blasted down the tunnel into cars in a tunnel below. The cars haul the ore out to the mill where the mineral content is extracted and the residue left as sand. It is a cheap method of mining and is employed in many parts of the world. In Colorado, molybdenum mining at Climax is a good example.

Returning to the Glory Hole above Central City (reached either from Nevadaville or off the Russell Gulch road). It is really the symbol of a period in Central City's history which began in 1927 and is perhaps not yet ended. Maybe it's a good period, or a bad one, depending upon whom you ask.

In 1923, mining production in Gilpin County had dropped to $85,526 from a peak of $3,359,240 in 1871, and it continued to fall. In 1927, the Chain O' Mines of Evanston, Illinois, was formed for the purpose of mining and milling the complex mineral deposits of Quartz Hill and other areas of the county.* It was all based on mining large quantities of low-grade rock by an economical mining method—glory holing.

A detailed story of the operation since 1927 would fill many books. It has had up and downs for nearly thirty-five years. At first, the project gave the community a shot in the arm: It provided employment, stimulated trade, reopened buildings long vacant, and caused a flourish if not a revival in the camp, that was sustained until the renaissance began with the annual Festival.

There is other evidence of this mining enterprise around Central City and Black Hawk—the mill, the pumping station on Clear Creek, the power line over Mammoth and Central Hills; most of all, the sand pile of mill tailings which, like a lava flow, was for awhile gradually creeping into town. (Mill tailings is the sand or residue left after minerals have been extracted from the finely ground rock.) In the triangle between Spring and Nevada Streets, the railroad depot is buried under the sand.

## 24. The City Park

Within the triangle formed at the intersection of Spring and Nevada Streets, a grandstand and a ball park were laid out in 1890. According to the local newspaper of June 19, 1890, "the grandstand in City Park

---

*Dr. William C. Muchow conceived the grand plan for the Chain O' Mines, and has sustained the idea for these many years.

24

will be completed in time for the baseball game between the Athletic Club and the Mays (May Company, Denver, team)."

The grandstand and home plate occupied the lower end of the park, with the bases lined up on Nevada and Spring Streets. Beyond the outfield, a new railroad station was being erected in August, 1899. The station also housed the Gilpin Tramway Company offices but was abandoned by the railroad in the early 1920's. In 1928, the building was leased to the contractors building the Chain O' Mines mill which was to produce the sand tailings that eventually buried it.

Now the station is covered and the old ball park serves as a parking lot.

## 25. The Old 71

Old 71, the newspaper called her, left Denver on the morning of April 10, 1941, for a one-way trip to Black Hawk, Central City, and history. The brightwork shined, the drivers and trim stood out in white, and the rest of her had a new coat of engine black. A picture taken alongside the roundhouse before departure showed that in this finery she was fairly prancing to be off on the familiar Clear Creek Canon trip, her last one.

No. 71 pulled two ancient cars, also heading for their last resting place: No. 4319, an ore carrier or gondola, and a baggage-coach or combination car, No. 20. The combo, of mid-1870 vintage, weighed 16 tons and, with a coal stove and coal oil lamp, could accommodate 16 passengers with a certain amount of comfort.

When the train reached the end-of-track at Black Hawk, the engine and cars were loaded on flat-bed trailers and hauled ignominiously to a final standing track in front of the old depot in Central City. Although Central City had been the terminus for many years, the track over the switchback between Black Hawk and Central City was taken out in the 1920's as the first step in abandonment of the entire road. So No. 71 and cars had to be hauled from Black Hawk to Central City by the very machine that had aided the abandonment.

A veteran Colorado and Southern crew brought the train to Black Hawk: J. W. Caragher, engineer; Martin Garrity, fireman; T. D. Brown, conductor; David Duggan, Sam Griffin, and Frank Weller, all brakemen.

A track crew came up from Denver to set up the engine and two cars alongside the old station. (The newer Central City depot, used but a short time before abandonment of service between Black Hawk and Central City, is buried under the sand tailings across the road.)

The train was purchased by the Opera House Association and properly dedicated to history on July 5, 1941. That was commendable because railroad service (No. 71's train wasn't quite the last) was discontinued on Sunday, May 4, 1941, 69 years after the first train entered Black Hawk.

The old roadbed between Black Hawk and Golden can be seen many places in Clear Creek Canon although the highway is built over it on some long stretches. Traces of the switchback and highline between Black Hawk and Central City are also easily discernible. (Incidentally, the highline provides an easy and interesting four-mile walk for anyone so inclined.) Picture takers who have trouble photographing No. 71 because of the fence around the train can blame the usual vandalism for this difficulty.

Here is a railroad timetable a traveler of 1906 would use between Denver and Central City, and from Central City to Denver:

### Denver to Central City

| Miles | *153 | *151 | STATIONS | *154 | *152 |
|---|---|---|---|---|---|
|  | 3:20 P.M. | 8:10 A.M. | Lv. Denver | Ar. 5:35 | 9:40 |
| 29 | 5:05 | 10:00 | Forks Creek | 4:10 | 7:49 |
| 34 | 5:24 | 10:19 | Smith Hill | 3:42 | 7:30 |
| 36 | 5:35 | 10:30 | Black Hawk | 3:32 | 7:20 |
| 40 | 6:00 | 10:55 | Ar. Central City | Lv. 3:10 P.M. | 6:55 A.M. |

* Daily

At Forks Creek, or Forks of the Creek, one branch of the railroad went to Central City and Black Hawk, the other to Idaho Springs and Georgetown, just as today route 119 branches off from U. S. 6 at the Forks. In those days, there were a pavillion and railroad offices at the Forks; today, nothing but a few signs.

Since Old 71 is a symbol of railroadism in Gilpin County, this is as good a place as any to mention other operating and proposed lines in the county.

In February, 1872, the Gilpin County Tram Railway Company was projected. It depended upon wooden rail, gravity, and horse power to move coal, wood, and ore. This was the forerunner of The Gilpin Tramway Company, organized in 1886, which used Shay engines on a two-foot track running from Black Hawk to the mines of upper Gilpin County. It provided a successful means of hauling ore down to the mills and railroad at Black Hawk, returning with coal and supplies for the mines. In the latter category was water, which was so scarce that it had to be hauled to some of the mines.

Writing of Gilpin County and the Gilpin Tramway, Frank Hall* said, "It has the only system of mining railway operated by steam power, whose trains run to and collect the marketabe ores from shafts and tunnels in all the region round about, delivering one class to the mills, and the other to the sampling works . . . transferring them via the Colorado Central Railroad to the smelters on the plains."

The Gilpin Tram's fortunes rose and fell with the production of ore from the mines. In 1906, the line became the Gilpin Railroad, a subsidiary of the Colorado and Southern Railway Company, and was dismantled in 1917.

The Virginia Tram Railroad Company was proposed on July 17, 1877, to run from Idaho Springs to the head of Virginia Canon, but nothing came of it. In 1907, the Pactolus Road, otherwise known as the Gilpin and Clear Creek District Railway, graded four miles out from Pactolus in South Boulder and then stopped cold. The intention was to build a standard gauge railroad into Gilpin and Clear Creek Counties from the Denver, Northwestern and Pacific Railroad, thus providing through service from Denver.

Lest any railroad buff object in the picture to the illusion of smoke coming out of 71's long-cold firebox and stack, it must be explained that a filter on the camera is to blame and, anyway, it's a pleasant illusion, some think.

---

*Frank Hall, *History of the State of Colorado*, 1889-1895.

25

25

26

49

George M. Pullman of sleeping car fame mined in Gilpin County in the early 1860's. Contrary to a persistant but incorrect legend, the Pullman car was not suggested by miners' bunks the inventor saw when he came to the mountains. Actually, he had a fleet of some dozen sleeping cars running on Eastern railroads before the Civil War.

## 26. The Hawley Warehouse

Construction on the Hawley warehouse was underway by November 29, 1877; an addition was built in December, 1881. In June of 1878, a telephone line connected warehouse and store on Main Street, a year before a public telephone system made a debut in Central City. This is not startling, though, because an intra-plant telephone was installed at the Black Hawk Sampling Works in 1877.

Hawley evidently believed in diversification as well as progress. In 1878, for example, the firm contracted to furnish 450 seats for the new Opera House. Three years later it was supplying Denver, Utah & Pacific grading camps over on South Boulder Creek with groceries and other necessities.

Zang Brewing Company of Denver built a warehouse alongside Hawley's, but it was torn down in 1920. The cribbing behind the warehouse was built by Nathaniel Batchelder, father of Mrs. Leroy Williams.

In 1881, the Hawley Merchandise Company had three establishments in Gilpin County. The business was closed out in 1936. (See Hawley Block.)

Presently the building is used for county highway maintenance shops.

## 27. Mason M. Seavy Block

The Seavy block was one of the few to escape the fire of 1874. A Collier photo, taken immediately after the fire, shows this building standing starkly by itself up at the end of Main Street. (In the same photo, the Roworth block on Main is also upright after the fire.)

The *Daily Register,* on September 19, 1868, said: "The first business block put up this season was that of Mason M. Seavy on the east side of Spring St. It is 25 by 65 feet on the ground and two stories high; the lower story 15 and the upper 12 feet high. Under the building is a cellar 30 feet square and 15 feet deep, which is a new thing for Central. With thick, substantial walls, tin roof and iron doors and shutters, the whole building is considered fireproof. But a thick fireproof wall dividing off the rear 25 feet of the lower story makes a room 25 feet square and 15 feet high almost absolutely fireproof. As Mr. Seavy was to occupy a block

27

28

29

himself with a storage, commission and grocery store, he told the workmen to spare no pains in making the first-class building which it is."

Notice the outside walls of this building which was one of the few
that survived the fire of 1874. The red color of the brick came from the
heat of the flames!

J. S. Beaman used the building as storage space for wines and liquors.
After that it was empty for nearly 40 years until converted into the Mining
and Historical Museum.

The next building, erected in 1881, has been used as Miller & Koch's
warehouse and as part of Beaman's bottling works. Above it is a structure
that survived the fire, as will be seen in the photo, which has been owned
by Henry E. Newcomb, and at another time by Harley Berky. Presently
it is a residence. The last building in the row has been a potato storage
warehouse.

## 28.  The Sauer-McShane Mercantile Warehouse

Of the three merchandise warehouses along Spring Street and bordering
the railroad tracks, the Sauer-McShane is the newest. An item in the
*Weekly Register-Call* of July 31, 1886, stated that workmen were erecting
a retaining wall on the M. H. Root lot on Spring Street preparatory to
the erection of a large warehouse. A second story was added ten years
later. An early day Central City lock-up is adjacent to the warehouse.

The main Sauer-McShane Mercantile Company store was located in the old Roworth block on Main Street. The name, before it was changed, is readily discernable on the building front.

## 29. Mellor & McFarlane Building

In the summer of 1875, the team of Mellor and McFarlane began building at the intersection of Spring and Gregory Streets. The foundation walls were laid by the end of July. Early in September it was reported that "the handsome iron fronts of Mellor & McFarlane buildings are in place, and the second floors of both buildings are making rapid progress." (This Mellor is believed to be John Mellor, the banker.)

The buildings were ready for occupancy by the middle of November. (One wonders why the asymetric shape of two structures built at the same time.) William Trounstine, clothing merchant, was to occupy one space; B. F. Pease, the other. Early in January of 1876, the Knights of Pythias had "fitted a cozy room in the McFarlane building."

The larger of the two was used for a decade or so in the late 90's by the Mueller Commission Co. Somewhere around 1901 it was taken over by Angelo Balaria for his Central Bottling Works. That same year the adjacent building was known as the Willis House, a rooming establishment. Of the three structures grouped together in what might be called a state of disrepair, the one farthest up the street was used by the telephone company as a supply store room before 1910.

## 30. 31. 32. The Parteli Block

Down at the end of Main Street, next to the Dostal block, the Parteli block is one of the newest additions to the Central City business district. Old photos show that the Temple of Fashion once stood on this site.

By 1897, there was a vacant lot here that sold "to persons unnamed for $1500." In March of that year, a contract was let for construction of "a two-story brick." The owner, then revealed as the Phillip Zang Brewing Co. of Denver, leased the premises to Bart Parteli and Gus Bensel, doing business as the Gold Coin bar. This name has been retained since 1897; now the business is run by heirs of Parteli. During prohibition, it was kept open as a pool hall and grocery store, and was operated in the latter category until 1943.

It is interesting to note that the building is bowed slightly toward the center, a situation caused by settling on the talc formation upon which it was built. The bar in the house was brought from Toledo to Denver by

ox team, and the flooring had been in place for 35 years in a Denver warehouse before being brought to Central City.

The Rock Shop, an adjunct owned by the Parteli heirs, was built by them in 1953. The Old Homestead is under the same ownership but takes the name from the Denver bakery that used to send up bread goods to Central City by train.

### 33. The Dostal Block

After the fire in 1874, three Central City merchants, described as "three of our most prosperous, worthy and industrious German citizens," made joint plans for the future. J. O. Dostal, Andy Bitzenhofer, and Frank Weisenhorn pooled capital and interests and built the 50 by 69-foot Dostal block at a cost of $3,000.

The center store in this block was occupied by Dostal's meat market, another by Henry Goetz's billiard parlor and lunch room, and the third Andy took for his "resurrected" Empire bakery. In August, 1875, he sold out to Ihrig & Reed but not before advertising "fresh, warm bread at Andy Bitzenhofer's in the basement of the new Dostal building."

On January 3, 1876, Dostal, too, pulled out of the entente, selling his meat market to P. G. Shanstrom who also had a market in Nevadaville. Dostal became a rancher in eastern Colorado.

Pictures taken in the 1880 era show that Aitcheson, a manufacturing jeweler, was located in the Dostal block. At another time, T. and Henry Dennis had a meat market here.

## 34. The Shaffnit Block

It would be easy to identify the Shaffnit block simply as the Quiller block, which it has been for 60 years; but that would be too easy, and inaccurate.

Before the fire, the Rocky Mountain National Bank occupied this site. After the flames destroyed the structure, instead of rebuilding here, the bank moved to the Teller House at the corner of Pine and Eureka Streets.

The *Weekly Register-Call* of June 2, 1878, reported that "Henry Shaffnit is grading the lot purchased from the Rocky Mountain National Bank and erecting a two-story building on it." Seemingly it was finished by November of that year because the word was out that "Joseph Tishler is moving into the Shaffnit block on Main Street."

There is a missing link between Tishler's tenancy here and Quiller's purchase of the building in 1900. Before his death in January, 1961, Earl Quiller, son of one of the founders of the firm, was of the opinion that Huber & Sons had a meat market here for many years, up until 1900. Then, and for ten years or so, it was William Quiller and Max Gabardi, continuing a meat market as Quiller & Gabardi, and then Quiller alone as a grocery and market. Before buying the corner building, Quiller was first in the Granite House and then the Elks block.

## 35. The Harris Block

At the corner of Main and Gregory Streets, though not bearing the family imprint, was built the second of three Harris blocks erected on Main Street. The June 14, 1878, issue of the *Weekly Register-Call* reported that "Thomas Mullen has a contract for the new Harris block on Main Street."

More is known about later tenants of this building than of those who occupied it after it was erected. For instance, this was once known as the Knights of Pythias building. (At one time, the lodge was housed in the building at Spring and Gregory Streets; at another, in the block on Lawrence Street now lettered KNIGHTS OF THE GOLDEN EAGLE.)

Benight's furniture and carpet store once used this ground floor corner, sharing the front with Day's drug store. In May, 1906, according to the *Weekly Register-Call*, "C. W. Knox opened a branch store in the Harris building for the sale of hoists, boilers, pumps and other mining machinery."

Around 1917, the pool hall of Kimball, Mitchell and Cecerro was installed here. In later years, the building has been used for basketball games and dances, and as a bowling alley and movie house in the 1940's.

## 36. The Hense Block (Main Street)

Toward the end of September in 1875, it was reported that the foundation walls of Hense's new building on Main Street were being laid, 22 feet wide, 60 feet deep. The two Hense buildings, one on Lawrence and one on Main Street, were once connected but the doorway has now been sealed.

Huber & Gebhart established a market here in 1876. Thomas Mullen was "digging a cellar next to Huber & Gebhart's" the week of June 14, 1878, preparing to erect the Harris block. For many years after that it was used for a saloon. It was also known as the Huber block.

## 37. The Miller Block

This corner was first known as the Miller block, later called Goldman's, and at various times bore a series of hotel names. As the Miller block, construction was begun in July, 1874, and finished in November at a cost of $8,000. (No information about Miller was found; he was possibly a James Miller described by Hall as a Central City pioneer.)

Note that the present hotel layout was made by joining the Bacharach and Hense buildings on Lawrence with the Miller building at the corner.

The Miller block or building fronted 55 feet on Lawrence and 50 feet on Main Street. The first three ground-floor tenants to occupy Miller's were D. C. Collier & Co., Samuel J. Marshall, and L. Alexander. The *Register* described a "spacious cellar beneath the entire building for the storage of goods. Eight rooms on the second floor are occupied by physicians, dressmakers and residential tenants."

While D. C. Collier was a lawyer, and had an office upstairs, he was also D. C. Collier & Co., the merchant. The firm was billed as "a branch of Gallup's renowned Denver Palace Bazaar . . . and the first store to receive customers after its completion. The 30 by 40-foot store is filled with a complete assortment of dress goods, notions and novelties."

Samuel J. Mitchell, a grocer, occupied No. 2 Miller block while Alexander, a "bottled goods merchant," was the third ground-floor tenant. Upstairs, a Miss Neyler had a millinery and dress making shop, and Drs. McMurtrie and Marsh, in separate rooms, received the ill and injured.

38                     37                                36        35

Collier moved his Bazaar to the Register block in December of 1875. By 1877, Beck & McMorran were conducting a drug business in the Miller building as were the jewelers, Hatch & Valentine.

Old photos show a variety of signs over the corner entrance. One was MILLER BLOCK; another, GOLDMAN'S, and still another, NEW HOTEL. And, at one time, it was known as the Central City Hotel.

For many years Elias Goldman ran a saloon known as Goldman's Corner in the building. A September, 1911, issue of the *Register-Call* said that, after 43 years in business, Goldman was selling out and going east to live. Came the first of Central City's twentieth-century revivals and the building became the Chain O' Mines Hotel. Just prior to that, upon the word of a Central City native, the building was tenanted for a long time by stray burros seeking shelter from the elements.

On April 15, 1896, the upstairs was the scene of a shooting that took place in true Western tradition. One J. M. Covington, an ore hauler, came up the stairs (the Main Street side) bent on bodily damage upon the person of Judge J. M. Seright, a lawyer with offices on the second floor, for an aggravated grievance. City Marshall M. F. Keleher, coming to Seright's assistance, stopped Covington's first bullet. Sheriff R. B. Williams stopped the second shot, which proved fatal. A lynching was averted when the murderer obligingly died while being taken to the jail.

In May, 1940, the name was changed from Chain O' Mines Hotel to Mines Hotel.

## 38. The Hense Block (Lawrence Street)

The first block below the main Mines Hotel building on Lawrence Street, but which is now part of the hotel, was built by John Hense shortly after the fire in 1874. Hense was a Central City jeweler and also the county treasurer. He erected the other Hense block on Main Street the following year. The two Hense blocks were connected by a corridor for many years but this is now sealed.

At the Lawrence Street building, one side of the first floor was the jewelry store where Hense was "a dealer in diamonds, rubies, emeralds, cameos, gold and silver." The other ground-floor space was rented to Neuman & Folster, who operated a bakery and grocery. Upstairs, Alex Carstens and Julius Strehlke had "one of the largest billiard halls in the west . . . four beautiful J. M. Brunswick tables." Receipts from this enterprise averaged $1,000 per month, the paper reported. The partnership was dissolved February 25, 1875, and Carstens carried on alone.

Hense died March 22, 1876, at the age of 42. The lower floor was then occupied by "W. Sauer, Furniture and Undertaking," and the upstairs by "J. Smallwood, Tailor."

The Hense block ran the full gamut of assorted occupants: bakeries, restaurants, clothing stores, and always, saloons. John Tague's place was here from about 1900 to 1907.

The Hense, Bacharach, and Miller blocks, constituting the hotel, were purchased in 1947.

## 39. Sol Bacharach's Block

Not all of the new "blocks" were built in Central City in 1874, the year of the fire. Sol Bacharach's new building, the second below the Miller block on Lawrence Street, was completed in September, 1875. It is presently the third unit of the hotel.

Upon completion, Robins & Search moved in with a fruit store while Bacharach occupied the other ground-floor side and dispensed wines and liquors. The upstairs rooms were used for living quarters as were many of the upper floors of buildings around town.

In January, 1876, Mrs. Phillip Gleason was running a "restaurant and

| 40 | 39 | 38 | 37 | 6 |

oyster saloon" in one of the two stores. (Oysters were featured the year around in Central City's markets and eating places.)

Sometime in the next two decades that followed, ownership of the Bacharach building passed to E. W. Williams and Bacharach remained as a tenant. Then Josiah Polglase bought the property and Bacharach moved out, first across Lawrence Street and then up to the post office building. In the early 1900's the bakery of Scheffler & Owen was located here.

Then there was the customary flow of businesses and vacancies in the Bacharach building until it became part of the hotel in the early 30's or before. In later years, the venerable Billy Hamilton, keeper of the Opera House keys, lived here until his death in November, 1960.

Once William Hoefle's gambling palace was located in the building.

## 40. Livery and Blacksmith Shop

It is said that this livery and blacksmith shop was built by R. B. (Dick) Williams, later proprietor of Williams' Stables across from the Teller House. Other smiths in here were Adolph Fuelscher, Elias Snyder, and Jim Barbee.

Below and across Spring Street, the Eclipse Stables owned by C. G. Wilcox, and at another time by Mayhew, stood for many years before being removed to make room for the school gymnasium.

## 41. The Dorris Building

This little building was not always as isolated as it seemingly is today. It is one of the newer structures, relatively speaking, and when built was surrounded by buildings that have disappeared with the passing of time. What occupied the site originally is not known.

On July 23, 1897, the *Weekly Register-Call* reported that James Dorris had put a force of men to work on his new Gregory Street building opposite the Welch building.

About 1898, Fritz Altvater purchased the *Gilpin County Observer* then being published at another small building on Main Street next to the O.K. (now known as A.O.U.W.) building. Shortly thereafter, the publication was moved to the building now designated as the Pink House, sharing space either then or later with the Chamber of Commerce. Altvater sold the *Observer* to W. J. Stull, who was publishing it as late as 1910, if not later.

Since then the building has had a variety of uses: gambling hall, Boy Scout gymnasium, school lunch room, perhaps some vacancies, and not a few times as collateral for loans.

Stull was sued in July of 1910 for $20,000. He once remarked that he would feel lonesome if a week should pass without a summons of some kind.

## 42. Dillon's

Down Lawrence Street, standing by itself, is the lone, stone building that once housed Dillon's saloon. Legend has it that when the establish-

41

ment was in full bloom, a sign warned the thirsty traveler that here was "The Last Chance Going Down," or "The First Chance Going Up," as the case might be.

## 43. 44. The Schools

The granite schoolhouse on First High Street, alongside the Episcopal Church, was one of the first two permanent schoolhouses built in Colorado, each in 1870. Central City's cost $20,000. The other, the frame building in Black Hawk, $15,000. One might think that construction costs would have been low in those days. The railroad didn't reach Denver until 1870, so much of the hardware and supplies were freighted across the plains by team, a costly factor.

In the fall of 1862, the first school of the area was a private one conducted by Miss Ellen F. Kendall in her father's log cabin. About the same time, a school board was created composed of D. C. Collier, Hiram A. Johnson, and A. Jacobs. Collier was elected superintendent. With a tax-raised $600, they opened a school later that year in Lawrence Hall with Thomas J. Campbell as principal and Miss Kendall his assistant. James C. Scott succeeded Campbell after the first term. By 1864, M. A. Arnold, Mrs. Arnold, W. F. Richardson, and John L. Schellinger were the teachers.

In the spring of 1868, school was conducted in what had been a "whiskey den and bowling alley" across from the Register block. Horace M. Hale and Mrs. James Burrell were the teachers.

Central City approved a $15,000 bond issue in April, 1869, for construction of a 240-student school which was completed in time for the opening of school in September, 1870. On the opening morning, 213 students answered the summons of a 400-pound bell mounted in the belfry. By then, Horace M. Hale was the principal, continuing in that post for several years until he was appointed territorial superintendent of public instruction. (Later, in 1888, Hale was elected president of the new state university at Boulder where Hale Hall on the campus was named in his honor.)

By 1880, a separate high school was needed in Central City. The old Congregational Church was used for a number of years as a high school until the new Clark grade school was built in 1900. Then the granite building became the high school. In 1930, it was designated a county high school when consolidation began. Armory Hall on Main Street was used for athletics. The present circular-roofed school gym stands on the site occupied for many years by the Eclipse livery stable.

43

46

47

44

45 48

49

42

## 45. St. Paul's Episcopal Church

The first Episcopalian Church in Central City was a wooden structure built on Lawrence Street in 1863 by George Randall. Bishop Randall was the missionary bishop of Colorado from 1865 to 1873. On the night of Sunday, January 28, 1873, a fire started in a faulty flue in the church and spread into the Central City fire that was the curtain riser for the Big Fire of the following year. The furnace in the building was the first hot air heater in the mountains.

The present Episcopal Church in Central City was started in 1873, finished in 1874, and consecrated the same year by Bishop William Spalding. (In 1874, the Episcopal Church had two stone buildings in Colorado, one in Central City, the other at Colorado Springs, each costing $10,000.)

St. Paul's, Central City, was organized in 1860, under Joseph C. Talbot, missionary bishop of the Northwest from 1859 to 1865. Rev. Thomas B. Newby was the first rector.

## 46. Raynold's Beehive

The Raynolds building withstood the onslaught of two fires, and was dubbed "beehive" because it sheltered businesses burned out by the second fire. Here, built in the 1860's, was the home and office of J. O. Raynolds, agent in Colorado for the Hazard Powder Company.

The first fire, starting in a bad flue in the old St. Paul's Church on Lawrence Street on the night of January 26, 1873, destroyed 16 buildings before it was stopped at Raynolds. Mrs. Raynolds hung water-soaked blankets and other wet cloth articles around doors, window frames, and other wooden surfaces to suppress the spread of fire. Her action not only stopped the flames but saved her cherished piano and prevented the detonation of whatever black powder may have been stored in the building.

This fire was bad enough but not of sufficient intensity to arouse the citizenry into providing adequate fire protection for the town. One branch of the fire of the following year, the big one of 1874, was also stopped on Lawrence Street, either at the Raynolds building or ahead of it. Mrs. Raynolds took the same precautions she had used the previous year.

About this, the *Register* said: "Owing to the wise precaution taken by J. O. Raynolds [no credit to Mrs. Reynolds], chief agent in Colorado for the powder company, their property has twice escaped fire."

After the second fire, numerous burned-out merchants found sanctuary in the Raynolds building when it literally became Raynolds beehive.

Witness: "At one time after the fire Raynolds' office and warehouse furnished accommodations for one bank [The First National], several mining companies, a meat market [Dostal], a boot and shoe store [Schwender], and a clothing store [O. K. Clothing], while what space that was left went to the dogs and cats. Raynolds' patience found a limit when somebody wanted to crowd a variety show on top of all others."

Even the city council for a time after the fire met at the Raynolds building.

The brick used is of a size and shape unmatched elsewhere in Central City, and it is conceivable that it may have been brought in from a considerable distance, perhaps even from overseas.

While Raynolds Beehive is generally credited with stopping the fire on that side of Lawrence Street, account must also be taken of the fact that Freas' "fireproof" building (now labeled KNIGHTS OF THE GOLDEN EAGLE) also stood up against the flames—before the fire reached Raynolds.

## 47. The Granite House

L. M. Freas came to Gregory Gulch with the 59'ers toting "a carpet bag and $5,000 worth of groceries and mining supplies." (The carpet bag part was probably said with tongue in cheek.) Freas first displayed his goods in a log cabin on the site later occupied by Raynolds Beehive. Freas then bought the lot next west and set up an establishment which became a victim of the fire in 1874. It was the last structure on Lawrence Street to be leveled by the flames before the fire was stopped by the fireproof Beehive.

Immediately after the fire, Freas started on the new granite-front building, 70 feet long by 50 feet deep. It was finished in December, 1874, at a cost of $14,000, and contained three "commodious" storerooms at ground level. The first was occupied by Charles Wentworth's hotel office and dining room; the next by Charles Tishler; the last by Will Nicholson's meat and vegetable market. The second was used for hotel rooms.

Charles Wentworth's first appearance as a landlord in Central City was in 1868 as proprietor of the Conner House. (This was the inn that Frank C. Young wrote "could not be said to be inviting in either its inner or outer respects. It served its purpose well enough in log cabin days. . .")

But better times were at hand. Wentworth's new Granite House in Freas' new granite building was described in this fashion by an enthusiastic *Register* reporter:

The Granite House . . . is a two story stone structure of substantial appearance, well calculated for small business. It has 11 good-sized sleeping apartments, all neatly furnished, and a cozy little parlor embellished with a Brussels carpet. Elaborate appointments include an Arion piano, pronounced by connoisseurs to be the best in the country. Has 19 regular boarders and as much transient trade as can be handled.

Here is a typical Granite House ad (February 8, 1875):

Hot supper tonight at the Granite House. Roast turkey and oysters of all styles. Charlie will have enough for all hands.

(This is a good time to talk about oysters—and Central City. In the early days, every eating place in town featured oysters: fried, raw, stewed, scalloped, and "all styles." In 1872, the railroad came to Black Hawk, which was about four hours from Denver, which, in turn, was many days and thousands of miles from the nearest oyster beds. Centralites had a tremendous appetite for oysters, satisfied, it seemed, by every cafe and market. How the oysters were handled and refrigerated is a story in itself. So good was the wholesale and retail oyster business that sales representatives—oyster drummers, if you will—could be put on the road, indicating that it was also probably a very competitive line. The newspaper, in November of 1881, noted that "a traveling agent for the Mallory brand of D. D. Mallory's brand of celebrated oysters was in town.")

Charlie stayed at the Granite House until January of 1877. From then on, according to newspaper accounts, there was a steady stream of landlords trying to make a go of it. (Somebody said there were a considerable number of suicides in the place. Perhaps that had something to do with it, or the other way around.)

In later years the building has been used mostly as a garage.

## 48. Knights of the Golden Eagle Building

This building predates the fire of 1874, although it is generally believed that Raynolds Beehive was the structure that finally stopped the fire on that side of Lawrence Street. In support of the foregoing satement about the age of this building, the *Register* of June 9, 1874, reported: "L. M. Freas let contract for a building between his fireproof and Raynolds." And later, speaking of Freas: "He has a two-story fireproof which passed through the fire untouched . . . immediately after the fire, Freas started a new building, granite front. . ."

The "fireproof" (building) of Freas, mentioned above, is only faced with brick. The main building material is stone. This may have been Freas' method of erecting a building.

65

Otto Sauer first rented the Freas building on Lawrence Street around April 22, 1881. The Emmet Guards, company A, 1st battalion, Colorado National Guard, leased the hall on December 21, 1881.

A 1900 fire insurance map of Central City shows that a grocery store occupied the lower floor, a Knights of Pythias lodge in the upper story. Going back to late 1885, an item in the *Weekly Register-Call* states: "Otto Sauer has leased a large room over the Sauer-McShane warehouse on Lawrence Street to Knights of Pythias No. 5 as a lodge room." How long this organization stayed in the building is not known. It is believed by some persons that the K. of P. may have been here only until 1900 and was then succeeded by the Knights of the Golden Eagle Star of the West Castle No. 3 who used it until—well, some say 1910, others claim it was used for lodge purposes until the early 1920's.

While in disuse for a long time, this venerable structure has come upon better times again. Early in 1961, it was purchased for use as a fire house, replacing the one in Washington Hall up Eureka Street. Besides the obvious advantage of being in a more strategic location from the standpoint of getting to a fire, one other very important fire-fighting factor accrues from stationing the fire equipment here! This is an interesting one: The Central City fire fighters are volunteers. Washington Hall is a good up-hill run for most of them. Now, with the fire house down grade for most of them—well, you see how it would be. . . .

## 49. Cessario's

The name is about all that can be told of this building at this time. Until more information is uncovered, all that is known is that this was Tony Cessario's saloon around 1908, give or take a few years. At one time, apparently in the late 90's, this was known as Vallero & Ebli's Vienna saloon. During depression days the building was used as a commodity warehouse.

## 50. The Hardware Store

The hardware store building on Lawrence Street, begun soon after the fire, was completed December 1, 1874. Going back before that, the firm of Ladd & Schuyler had been established in Black Hawk in 1869. Shortly after the fire, the partners bought a lot on Lawrence Street and immediately began erection of a "fireproof store and a copper and tin factory." (In those days many kitchen and household wares were turned out in small manufactories such as this.) An $8,000 stock of stoves and hardware was put into inventory, in addition to the repair and manufacturing

facilities. The building measured 28 by 63 feet on the ground level, but was 22 feet deeper on the second floor.

Write the *Register* reporter about Ladd & Schuyler's new building: "It is intended to be as fireproof as human skill, with due regard to architectural symmetry, can make it." The firm reported a gross business of $35,000 for 1874, which doubtless included earnings at the Black Hawk store. In September, 1881, Root & Sears were building the new Ladd & Schuyler warehouse adjacent to the store.

Dave Henderson, Dan McKay, and John Jenkins bought out Ladd & Schuyler in 1887. John Jenkins was a several-times mayor and alderman of Central City, as has been his son, John Jenkins, Jr., present head of the company, which in 1922 purchased the Clark hardware store in Black Hawk

Dave Henderson was credited with many inventions, and the production of numerous mechanical items which found world-wide use and acceptance. A stamp mill screen, for example, was sent into mining camps all over the world. This and other mechanical devices were the product of a punching machine, invented and perfected by Henderson, that turned out screens of any required mesh. Kidney-shaped lunch buckets, favored by the Cousin Jack miners because they were made to accommodate Cornish pasties, were also a production item of the shop.

## 51.  Edmundson Block III

This is the third of three buildings built by Dr. William Edmundson on Lawrence Street for investment purposes. The three extended from the Golden Rule store in the Hanington & Mellor block down to the hardware store.

About this block, the *Weekly Register-Call* of August 30, 1880, said: "Dr. Edmundson has let a contract for grading off lots between Ladd & Schuyler's and Sol Bacharach's on which to erect a block of building to be 50 feet by 72 feet to be divided into three business or store rooms. Thomas Mullen is doing the work."

Dr. Edmundson moved to Denver in 1880, and before the end of the year became chairman of the Colorado State Board of Health. He was a Civil War veteran, and practiced medicine in Denver for many years after leaving Central City.

This building has housed the usual run of businesses but, specifically, it has been occupied by a shoe repair shop, and, naturally, by a saloon. Twice tax deeds have been issued for it, and once it was used to help secure $150,000 worth of bonds. It has been a hotel annex, a newspaper plant, a harness shop, and a tea and coffee store.

It wouldn't be fair to reveal any figures but the present owner says he paid more for the abstract than he did for the property. And that isn't at all surprising when you consider the value of Central City property back in depression days.

## 52.  The Edmundson Block II

Here is the second of three investment properties built by Dr. William Edmundson, Central City physician and public-spirited citizen of the 1870's. Dr. Edmundson moved to Denver in 1880, practicing there until his retirement around 1917.

The *Weekly Register-Call* on July 12, 1878, reported: "Dr. Edmundson is letting a contract for the erection of a three-story building on the lot adjoining his block on Lawrence Street." Sol Bacharach had given up the wine and beer establishment in his own building across Lawrence Street and was one of the first tenants in the new block. Also, it was planned that the city offices would be in this new building, but this move apparently didn't take place. This block is three stories high only in the front part.

## 53. The Edmundson Block I

The three buildings, or blocks, between the Mellor block and the hardware store were erected as an investment by Dr. William E. Edmundson, a practicing physician and prominent citizen of Central City. The doctor came to Gilpin County in 1868 after serving in the Civil War. He moved to Denver in 1880, retiring from practice in 1917.

The *Weekly Register-Call* on April 7, 1877, reported that "Dr. Edmundson will begin erection of a two-story building in the lot next below Hanington & Mellor's banking establishment . . . N. A. Sears has the contract for construction." This building is obviously a three-story and from the following it seems certain that the doctor changed his mind and decided upon a larger building. On June 2, 1877: "Workmen on the three-story Edmundson block on Lawrence Street. . . ."

Dr. Edmundson's obituary printed July 17, 1929, noting his death at the age of 87, stated that the Edmundson block in Central City included those buildings from the Golden Rule store (Hanington & Mellor block) to the hardware store. The next two Edmundson buildings were erected in July, 1878, and in August, 1880. Dr. Edmundson was a Gilpin County Opera House Association board member and a superintendent of the Central City schools.

As the plaque on the post office notes, Edmundson raised his new building on the site occupied before the Great Fire of 1876 by the Montana Theater.

Mention of the Montana brings up a story that cannot go untold. The incident could be something out of TV, common today on that media, but exceptional enough in the early 60's to warrant being recorded by Frank Hall, a great historian of those times.

The first theatrical offerings were given in the old Hadley cabin in Mountain City, the next community below Central City in Gregory Gulch. It was presented by the itinerant troupe of Madame Wakely and "the fascinating Haidee Sisters." Hall writes, "The next temple of Thespis was erected in Central City in 1862, by George Harrison, the survivor of one of the most thrilling tragedies in real life that has occurred here. It was christened the National." So much for the background.

Soon after his theater was finished, Harrison got into a quarrel with one Charley Switz, prize fighter and keeper of an unsavory saloon and variety show below the National on Lawrence Street. The row was stopped, but each participant vowed that it would be ended only by the man who could outdraw the other upon their next meeting.

Harrison left shortly after that "for the states" to bring out a new theatrical troupe. When his imminent return was rumored, Switz strapped on a brace of guns, repaired to Barnes & Jones' saloon for some liquid courage (just as it's done on TV). The saloon was situated between the National and Ben Holladay's stage office. The hangers-on smelled excitement and gathered for the fray. But Harrison left the stagecoach before it reached Central City. Sneaking around the back way with a loaded double-barrel shotgun, he mounted a balcony overlooking the street—and bad-man Switz. Getting a good bead on Switz, Harrison let go with both barrels of shot.

The affair over, Harrison walked calmly into his theater and began preparations for the grand opening. He was "arrested, but not confined, tried, but not convicted." The body of the loser was removed to his own saloon and "stripped, washed, and with nothing but a sheet to cover the ghastly remains, laid out for examination by the crowds that called."

54      53      52

Harrison finished the season at the National, sold out to Langrishe & Dougherty who rechristened it the Montana, and headed south to join the Confederate forces. So much for what happened in 1862 in front of the present Central City post office.

In September 1877, the paper reported "Two glass windows, 58 x 128 inches, were put into the new Edmundson block and are the largest in the mountains." That same fall, Western Union moved into an office upstairs. At another time Chase Withrow, the lawyer, had a second-floor office, too.

Occupying the ground level, there has been a meat market, M. B. Hyndman's book store, a candy store, and Joseph Kimball's pool hall. In 1880, Sol Bacharach moved in from across the street.

Chase Withrow died in January, 1931, at the age of 91. He was the last of 38 pioneers who journeyed to Denver in 1876 to help draft the new Colorado constitution. It was said that "his life virtually encompassed the growth of the state from pioneer times to the present."

Almost until the last few years, Mr. Withrow took an active part in public, legal, and fraternal affairs. He was the oldest member of the Masons in Colorado and past grand master of the organization in the United States.

He attended the Lincoln-Douglas debate, and in 1859 set out for the Rockies, settling in Central City where he studied law and was admitted to the bar in 1874. He became an authority on mining and agricultural law.

## 54. The Mellor Block

For many years the Mellor block housed the Hanington & Mellor bank, Central City's third banking institution, and the Kansas Pacific Express Co. Later the Golden Rule store occupied the building.

Before the fire in 1874, the Concert Hall and Bellaire rooms were on this site as was Warren Hussey's bank, founded in 1863, the forerunner of The First National Bank of Central City. Fire destroyed the building, but a huge inner vault remained intact.

After the fire, John Mellor and Henry Hanington started their private bank in the new Wells Fargo building when it was completed in 1874. (But shortly after the fire a *new Concert Hall* was erected on the site of the *old Concert Hall*, next to the Wells Fargo building. It was a temporary structure, put up to provide make-shift entertainment of a not too elegant nature until more permanent quarters became available. Besides, new post-fire regulations in Central City allowed only temporary wooden buildings. And make-shift it was because on January 4, 1875, an ad was

54

run announcing "a grand closing of the Concert Hall tonight," and elsewhere in the paper: "For sale—the frame building on Lawrence Street
known as Concert Hall—$200. Apply at office." If there were any takers
they were not mentioned. But obviously the lot was of great value.)

There was a rumor abroad in Central City on May 8, 1875, that "John
Mellor would build an elegant block on the site of the old Concert Hall
and Montana Theater as soon as title to the ground is cleared." Workmen were clearing away the rubble on the site by June 1, 1875, and the
paper said, "In a few months we shall see two handsome brick structures
occupying the ground from Wells-Fargo 72 feet down Lawrence Street."
On November 17 of that year Hanington & Mellor, bankers, and Robert
A. Campbell, agent for the Kansas Pacific Express Co., were installed in
the new Mellor block.

Hanington & Mellor voluntarily closed out the business of their bank
about 1889. Sometime thereafter the space was occupied by the Golden
Rule store. In 1876, Dr. W. H. Jackson was an upstairs tenant, which
portion, about 1900, became a sort of public reading room. At later dates,
the Mellor block was occupied by Pease & Co., Central Clothing, and
Red & White grocery store.

## 55. Wells, Fargo & Co.

Wells, Fargo & Co. was successor to John Sowers & Co., Hinckley, and Ben Holladay, the several express companies operating into Central City in the early days. When built, rising quickly from the ruins of 1874 the Wells, Fargo building was described as "small but with ample room for express consignments on the ground floor. Three well arranged rooms on the second floor are occupied by Dr. R. G. Aduddell, physician and surgeon."

Robert A. Campbell was agent for the company. Later he became representative of the Kansas Pacific Express Co. when it was installed, together with Hanington & Mellor's bank, in the Mellor block a few doors down Lawrence St. after that building was finished in 1875.

The original structure standing on this site before the great fire of 1874 housed the express office which was shared with George T. Clark's banking firm. It was here that Clark and other Gilpin County notables welcomed General Grant on his first trip to Central City in 1868. (On this occasion, the general is said to have remarked to Henry M. Teller that Central City badly needed a railroad, so rugged was the trip up from Denver. Teller later became president of the Colorado Central which served Gilpin County for many years.)

In 1875, after the building was vacated by the express company and Hanington & Mellor, Henry Goetz set up his casino here. After that it had the usual round of tenants.

By 1911, Wells, Fargo & Co. no longer operated in Central City.

## 56. The Pharmacy

This is the oldest drug store in Colorado. John Best, a native of England and graduate of the New York College of Pharmacy, came to Central City in 1864. He bought Ben Hay's drug store in the Gurney building "for less than $5,000."

When the great fire of 1874 struck, Best, it is told, just had time to chuck two or three flasks of mercury (used in the recovery of gold) down a well and flee the building. His store was "totally snuffed out." Best received some attractive offers to work in Denver, but after checking these out, he decided within 48 hours to remain in Central City.

Back in town he purchased "the grounds and smoking walls" next to Wells, Fargo & Co. Somehow he managed to install shelves and counters and immediately placed an order for goods with eastern suppliers. Within 30 days, foundations for "a new and elegant pharmacy" were laid. The

58 57    56         55                                                        54

building was finished in August of 1874: a "two story brick, iron front crowned by metallic cornices. The main storeroom is 25 x 30 feet. The upper story is divided into two compartments, one for an office, one for a storeroom. Stock is worth $12,000; the year's business in 1874, $40,-000."

On May 5, 1875, it was reported that "Best's soda fountain was just received from New York and is a beauty." The same year Best advertised "Quicksilver, acids, ammoniac oils, etc. for mine and mill at the Pharmacy."

In 1887, Best sold his pharmacy to Ll. P. Davis, and engaged in a mining enterprise (forsaking drugging for digging, so to speak). In 1897, a John Best was superintendent of the Saratoga mine. The following year his successor at the pharmacy, Dr. Ll. P. Davis advertised a new medicine that should have sold well in Central City: "The Miner's Drink, prepared for miners having miners consumption due to rock dust, powder fumes and bad air."

After Best, there have been only four owners of the Pharmacy. This, the newspaper, and the Teller House are the only businesses that have operated continuously since the early 1870's.

The iron front on Best's pharmacy was the first installed in Central City and set a precedent for others that followed on other buildings.

58   57   56     40 39 38

## 57. Harley B. Morse Block

The Morse block, or building, is on the site of the office and residence occupied by Harley B. Morse prior to the fire in 1874. The "judge" was a lawyer, mine owner, probate judge and a historical figure in Gilpin County affairs.

The original structure was a log cabin built in 1859. Because the fire was stopped on this side of Eureka Street by the fireproof Register block, Morse's cabin adjoining it was one of the last destroyed.

A newspaper account reported that Morse erected a single story brick building, the first in the city, by June 1, 1874, less than ten days after the fire. Upon completion, Messrs. Cohen & Bernstein moved in "with the only stock (clothing) of its kind left in the city." It was further stated that with this $15,000 stock the partners did a $40,000 business in 1874. The second story was added later in 1874, making the total cost of the building $3,000.

Thereafter, it was used for various businesses, as is the case with all Central City buildings. In 1951, the local mining industry, on the ropes and making a last stand (along with gold mining country-wide), opened for a while a mining chamber of commerce in the building. In the early days, James M. Seright also had a law office here.

The *Register*, in summarizing building activity for the year 1874, was very firm in stating that Morse's first building erected after the fire was a single story brick, to which the owner added the second story later in the year. The present owner, William C. Russell, Jr., has found no evidence of a second story being added to the first.

The newspaper issue of August 18, 1874, said that "Judge Morse should make arrangements for a two-story building uniform with John Best's." Then on October 9: "Judge Morse is preparing to put up a handsome two-story brick. . . ." Again on November 2, 1874: "Cohen & Berenstein have the only two-story clothing store in the city."

So it is possible that the single-story building Judge Morse erected right after the fire—"within nine days"—was unsatisfactory and had to be replaced with the two-story block we see today.

## 58. The Register Block

This venerable masonry structure, probably the oldest still in use in Central, must be regarded as having three distinct parts: the store fronts known as Nos. 1 and 2 on the street level, the *Weekly Register-Call* newspaper plant on the second floor, and the Masonic Temple on the third story.

The *Weekly Register-Call* is the second oldest continuously published newspaper in Colorado. (The *Rocky Mountain News* in Denver, founded by William N. Byers in 1859, is the oldest. In Gilpin County, The *Rocky Mountain Gold Reporter* and *Mountain City Herald* was printed in August, 1859. It ceased publication at the onset of winter but reappeared the following year in Denver as *The Rocky Mountain Herald*. The *Colorado Miner*, a weekly, made an appearance in Black Hawk in 1863, published by William Train Muir.)

The story behind the *Register-Call* and the Register block is one of evolution, and meetings of minds and pocketbooks. In the summer of 1862, Alfred Thompson brought a hand lever press, type, and other printing equipment to Central City from Greenwood, Iowa. On July 26 of that year he began publication of the *Miners' Register*. David C. Collier was hired as an editorial writer. He, Hugh Glenn, and George A. Wells bought the paper April 9, 1863. The next day it appeared as a morning paper with wire services. Glenn sold his interest to Collier and Wells on September 29 of that year.

In the winter of 1861-62, the Register block, less the third floor, was built, and on October 17, 1865, Wells sold his half interest in the paper to Frank Hall, a journalist and historian. It became the *Central City Register* July 12, 1873. Collier then sold out to W. W. Whipple, and before long Hall purchased Whipple's interest. Hall retained control until June 1 1877, when it passed to James A. Smith and Don Marlow. The paper was leased to Huley M. Rhoads on February 1, 1878. In February of that year G. M. Laird began publication of the *Evening Call,* and in May the two papers were combined into the *Register-Call,* Laird & Marlow, proprietors.

Rae Laird, present editor, publisher, and son of G. M. Laird, tells how imposing stones for the shop were brought across country by ox team; that during Indian troubles wallpaper and wrapping paper were sometimes used when a newsprint shipment was destroyed. But the newspaper has never missed an issue. Alfred Thompson's wood and metal type and press are still used occasionally. (See type used on cover of this book.)

The third floor was added in 1864 when the Masons of Chivington Lodge No. 6 united with Collier & Hall "and from their own means added the third story to the building." J. W. Chivington Lodge No. 6 was chartered by the Grand Lodge of Colorado December 11, 1861. The name was changed to Central Lodge No. 6 in 1866. A plaque on the building front tells more: "The Cradle of Masonry in the Rocky Mountains. Murals painted by candlelight in 60's are preserved . . . site revered by Masons from all parts of the world in annual pilgrimages to Central City." (John V. Glendenin painted the murals. He died at Evanston, Wyoming, in February, 1875.)

(John M. Chivington came to Colorado Territory in 1860 as a presiding elder of the Rocky Mountain district, Methodist Episcopal church. Although he lacked formal military training, in 1861 Governor Gilpin commissioned him a major in the 1st Colorado Cavalry. His participation in the battle of Glorieta Pass was brilliant and heroic. His later action at Sand Creek is, and probably will ever be, a matter of lasting controversy.)

As has been done in most other "store rooms" in town, the businesses of Central City have played a game of "musical chairs" in Nos. 1 and 2, Register block, for almost 100 years. Every enterprise imaginable has occupied the two spaces which share honors with Raynolds Beehive in that respect. Because these two buildings were untouched by the fire of '74, the burned-out merchants flocked to the Beehive and Register buildings to set up temporary quarters after the fire. In the case of the latter, there has been an unending stream of tenants ever since.

Here are a few of the early-day occupants: H. J. Kruse, groceries; Bon Ton restaurant; J. H. Schwender, shoes and boots; J. Collier's photographic studio, followed by L. McLain in the same line. Also Sessler & Sauer; the music hall of Schlessinger & Lintz, moving from the Alhambra; Lazares & Morris, jewelry and watch repair; and E. Goldman, the saloonkeeper. Also D. C. Collier, moving in from the Miller block. In 1877, E. H. Lindsey, proprietor of "The Elevator" in the Teller House, opened "The New State—the most attractive resort in the city" (a saloon) in the Register block. The parade goes on and on, indefinitely.

In 1890, the Masonic lodge of Central City purchased the two lower floors of the Register block for $6,000 from W. C. Fullerton. Rae Laird estimates a total of $132,000 in rent has been paid since 1864 by newspapers occupying the Register block.

Today, the following lodges meet in the Masonic rooms on the third floor of the Register building:

Central City Chapter No. 1, R.A.M. (2nd Monday each month)

Central Lodge No. 6, A.F. & A.M. (2nd and 4th Wednesday)

Central City Commandery No. 2 K.T. (Every 3rd Thursday)

Golden Queen Chapter No. 17, Order of Eastern Star (1st and 3rd Tuesdays)

Nevada Lodge, No. 4.

The second floor front rooms in the Register building have been occupied for many years by prominent lawyers of Central City: Leroy J. Williams, Kenneth Montgomery, and others.

## 59. Williams' Stables

On this site once stood an "unsightly log cabin" belonging to Henry M. Teller. It was one of the first buildings in Central City, but from all accounts its usefulness was over about the time of the fire of 1874. Early in February, 1876, Teller ordered the cabin demolished and made plans for "a handsome brick" in its place.

But, instead, the lot was purchased by a brother of W. H. Bush, the Teller House manager, on April 7, of that year. He announced grading would commence immediately for construction of a two-story brick and stone building to be used as a livery and stable "outfitted with a large lot of fine horses and carriages"— for Teller House guests.

Sheriff Dick Williams, while operating a livery just below Bacharach's block on Lawrence Street, purchased the stables in 1880. Then for 16 years he operated Williams' Stables until his death in 1896 of a gunshot wound. Oscar Williams, also a Gilpin County sheriff, succeeded his father in the business until 1913. In December, 1911, he purchased the stock and fixtures of the Eclipse Livery Stables (which was on the site now occupied by the School gymnasium) and ran it together with the Williams' Stables. Marshall's service garage was here in 1935 but the building, which now belongs to the city, is the scene of colorful square dancing each summer.

In July, 1915, Williams was advertising that a Stanley steamer was available for hire, which meant that Williams was a realist who kept up with the times in the livery business.

### 60. Henry M. Teller's Office

Erected in 1862 and now nesting between Washington Hall and Williams' Stables is the one-time law office used by one of Central City's most illustrious citizens. Although moved several times, to make room for the Teller House, and in later years for the opera annex, it is one of the oldest buildings in Central City. It, too, was protected from the fire in 1874 by the fire-resisting Teller House.

Henry M. Teller was born in Orleans County, New York, in 1830. He taught school for a spell and then studied law in Binghamton, New York. Coming to Colorado after a stop in Illinois, he settled in Central City, and in 1862 began the practice of law in this building. Soon he was engaged in the affairs of city, county, and territory.

Teller was the first president of the Colorado Central, the narrow-gauge railroad that in 1872 linked Gilpin County with the outside world. Among other activities, he was owner of the Teller House, president of the Rocky Mountain National Bank of Central City, and president of the Rocky

61          60          59

Mountain Telegraph Company which had expanded a line from Central City to Caribou to link with Boulder, Denver, Cheyenne, and the east.

On January 7, 1877, following Colorado's admission to statehood, Teller and Jerome B. Chaffee were elected to the United States Senate. Teller left to become Secretary of the Interior in the cabinet of President Chester Arthur, but returned and remained in the Senate until 1906. In politics, he broke with the Republicans over the silver question in 1896, leading a group of free silverites from the convention that year. It was said that he changed from a Silver Republican to a Bryan Democrat.

## 61. Washington Hall

This ancient, two-story frame was spared from destruction in the great fire of '74, only to be threatened by firebugs the following year. In 1874, the fire-resisting Register building stopped the flames on the east side of Eureka, but in January, 1875, arsonists were at work. Notices were out posting a reward of $290 "for the arrest and conviction of the party or parties setting fire to Washington Hall and adjacent properties."

This little gem probably comes as close to being a community hall for nearly 100 years as anything Central City ever had. The shell of the building is framed of logs in a structure erected in 1861. The siding was added about 1864.

Justice was dispensed with or without on the upper floor where, first, the Gregory Miners Court convened, and then the first district court of the Territory. County offices and the jail were on the ground floor.

Methodists and Presbyterians held services in the courtroom at various times. Once a congregation of the former heard their Rev. Mr. Adams on a Sunday in 1868 warn all evil doers to "flee from the wrath to come." Prisoners in the jail below heard the exhortation and fled the jail during the night, so the story goes.

Washington Hall's chief glory was as a political arena. One classic incident took place during a Republican convention in 1871, held in the upstairs courtroom. So great was the combined weight of the delegates that the floor gave way, pitching all and sundry to the center.

Washington Hall has been used on various state occasions, such as for the funeral of Mike Daugherty, the associate of Jack Langrishe, theatrical producer of the 60's and 70's. Since July 27, 1900, it has served as the city hall. From the beginning, the city halls had been makeshift affairs rented in various parts of town. When the county vacated Washington Hall for the new court house, the city fathers decided money could be saved by establishing permanent city offices in the old building.

64          63          62          61

## 62. Cast Houses

Two frame houses are used by members of the Opera House cast during the season. The lower, part frame and part brick, has been owned and occupied in the past by Dr. R. G. Aduddell, pioneer physician and surgeon of Central City, by Dick Williams, sheriff and operator of the Williams' stables, and by Harry Armfield.

To the rear and right of this house is a small, one-time dwelling now used by the city as a pipe shop.

Above the Armfield house is one owned as a dwelling for many years by Mrs. Maggie Ross, long-time milliner of Central City who for many years had a shop in the Teller House. Several years ago, while repairs were being made at the rear of the house, evidence was uncovered that indicated the building dates back at least to 1865. Beyond and to the left of the Ross house is a smaller and newer dwelling, also owned by Mrs. Ross.

## 63. St. James Methodist Church

St. James was organized July 10, 1859, by two missionaries, Rev. W. H. Goode and Rev. Jacob Adriance. It is the oldest Protestant Church organization, as well as the oldest Protestant Church building still in use, in Colorado. Rev. George W. Fisher, wagon maker and lay preacher, was the first resident pastor.

Land for the church was purchased in 1862, but construction did not start until 1864, during the pastorate of Rev. B. T. Vincent. Funds were exhausted before the building reached completion, and, with only the basement finished and the walls standing, the structure was known as "The Ruins."

Rev. G. H. Adams became pastor in 1867 and at once began a program for finishing the structure. In 1868, with funds on hand, it was found that the walls were unsuitable for the building. It then became necessary to start construction again from "the ground up." But when completed, the stonework was pronounced the best in the territory.

For awhile services were held in the home of Aunt Clara Brown, a former slave who bought freedom in 1857 and came to Central City in the '59 rush. At another time Washington Hall was used for a meeting place.

St. James was dedicated July 21, 1872, by Bishop R. S. Foster. It cost $35,000, one-half of which was paid by that date. By December, 1879, the church debt was lifted. In September, 1916, a mayor's deed was issued to the trustees of St. James in lieu of one misplaced. The pipe organ, dedicated November 5, 1899, cost $3,000, one-third provided by the heirs of Robert E. Harris. (The organ operated by water power until 1932.) In 1899, a $1200 heating plant was installed along with a new carpet which is in use today. The eighty oak pews provide a seating capacity of 400 persons and were also installed in 1899. But that isn't enough to accommodate the crowd that attends the annual homecoming, or anniversary, service each year held in memory of the dedication back in 1872.

## 64. The Gilpin County Court House

Gilpin County was named for William Gilpin, the first territorial governor of Colorado. He was appointed by President Lincoln and served from July 8, 1861 to April 19, 1862. The county was one of nine established by the provisional government of Jefferson Territory in 1859, and was then known as Mountain County. When Gilpin County was named by the territorial legislature in October, 1861, the name was not without opposition from partisans of John Gregory who insisted that the county be named for the discoverer of gold in the gulch. Had Gregory remained in the area, his proponents might well have succeeded in their plan to name the county for him.

But the Gilpinites won, and the first county commissioners were G. W. Jacobs, Archibald Van Deren, and Galen Norton.

For many years, most of the county business was conducted at Washington Hall on Lawrence Street. Finally, the need was recognized for a courthouse worthy of the name, and the voters authorized a $00,000 bond issue to finance a new building. The bonds were put up for sale March 27, 1897, in denominations of $1,000 each, payable after 10 years at 5% compounded semi-annually.

The county commissioners visited many of the county seats, looking for another, suitable courthouse to duplicate. The one selected was the Otero County courthouse at LaJunta, Colorado. Even so, the Denver architect firm of Baerrenson Bros. & Son was commissioned to draw the plans. Lamont & Ballard was the contractor, and Newton D. Owen, credited with building the Teller House, Episcopal Church, and others, the superintendent.

A progress report stated that "the foundation walls are three to four feet thick and 26 feet deep in back. The basement is of Ft. Collins stone two feet thick, and the building is of the best Golden brick."

Sometime after construction was started, a question arose about the legality of the bond issue and work was suspended for a time. The trouble straightened out, building resumed and the courthouse was turned over to the county February 20, 1900, in ceremonies capped by a dedication ball after a day of speech making.

Originally, the steps ran across more of the breadth of the building, but this was later modified. When the county offices vacated, Washington Hall was sold to Central City, and after 40 years of wandering around town city government had a home at last.

The courthouse stands on the site once occupied by the Henry M. Teller home. The father of William Ziege built the stone wall at the back of the courthouse.

## 65. Anne Evans Observation Point

The Anne Evans Point is reached from upper Eureka Street. The June 30, 1950, issue of the *Weekly Register-Call* said: "Anne Evans is to be honored July 4, with the dedication of an observation point at the foot of Bald Mountain facing Mt. Evans. The proposal to name the point in her honor was made by John Jenkins, Jr. and the county commissioners."

About Anne Evans, Caroline Bancroft writes in her *Gulch of Gold*, "Anne Evans had aided enormously in financing and in organizing the

65

66

Central City Opera House Association. . . ." Miss Evans, daughter of the second territorial governor of Colorado, died in Denver in January, 1941.

## 66. Mack's Rocky Mountain Brewery

The ruins of Jacob Mack's brewery are in evidence at the head of Eureka Gulch. In 1874, according to a newspaper account, the operation was "one of the most extensive in the territory" with a stock of merchandise valued at $10,000 and sales amounting to $18,000 per year.

In 1881, Mathias Mack supervised the business which was destroyed by fire in 1885 with a $12,000 loss. Jake, who in the meantime had gone over the mountains to establish another brewery in Leadville, returned to rebuild the Central City establishment after the fire. The layout had a beer garden with a ten pin lane.

## 67. The City Reservoir

The prominent Central City contractor, N. A. Sears, built this city water supply reservoir in Eureka Gulch, beginning in the spring of 1886. When completed, it provided, among other things, 110-pound water pressure at the hydrant on the First National Bank corner, 385 feet below the reservoir outlet.

67

(On the downhill side of the reservoir note the old railroad grade that swings around from the east, crosses Eureka Street just below the structure, and continues on around and up Gunnell Hill to the west. This is the remains of the old Gilpin Tramway line, a unique two-foot gauge railroad that hauled ore down from the mines to the mills scattered along Clear Creek in Black Hawk. Traces of the old grade can be seen and walked over at many places. It is visible suspended on rock walls over Chase Gulch, and overlooking highway 119 above and below Black Hawk. The tram, built in 1886, was dismantled in 1917 because of diminishing revenues.)

This reservoir is the largest of two, actually three, in Central City and was built to hold 16,800 barrels (apparently the measure of storage capacity in those days). Originally, water was drawn into it from springs on the Toinby, Tascher and Thompson ranches. The reservoir was put at this site because Jacob Tascher, who was also a water vendor delivering up to 100 barrels per day at 40c a barrel to householders, suggested that the city take over his quartz mill in Eureka Gulch and convert it into a reservoir. That was in 1875. The city finally did as he suggested, but not until 1886, and the project was financed with a bond issue.

The other reservoir located on Gunnell Hill near the Ida Kruse McFarlane Memorial predates the one in Eureka Gulch. In November, 1875, city council "let a contract for enlarging and refitting the reservoir on Mt. St. Vincent to Thomas Mullen." Actually, there was still a third storage reservoir, built in 1872 to supply the Teller House. In later years, it stored water for street flushing purposes.

Seemingly, not even three reservoirs were adequate because as late as July 20, 1900, water was advertised for sale at the city loading places for 25c a tank. There may have been enough water in storage but it wasn't getting into distribution. The water problem has always been a real time for Central City.

## 68. The Foundry

On upper Eureka Street are ruins of Colorado's oldest foundry built in 1881 by Hendrie & Butler, becoming Hendrie Bros. in 1864, and Hendrie Bros. & Bolthoff in 1873.

Although the foundry was untouched by the Great Fire of 1874 (it was the refuge of many who were burned out), the owners rebuilt it "on a more substantial and extensive basis." The capacity was enlarged "commensurate with the increasing needs of mining and manufacturing."

The new structure measured 50 by 30 feet, with an upper story for pattern making. The machine shop was equipped with lathes, drill presses, screw cutter, and iron planes. Altogether, "12 to 16 hands" were employed. The adjacent building was the moulding works where all casting was done.

On March 10, 1887, it was reported that "the copartnership between [sic] Charles F. Hendrie, William C. Hendrie and Henry Bolthoff has been dissolved, the contract expiring. The firm name of Hendrie Bros.

68

& Bolthoff will be continued by Charles F. Hendrie and Henry Bolthoff." The firm built and installed equipment for mines and mills locally and all over the country.

Later in 1877, the business was incorporated, along with the Denver part of the firm, as Hendrie & Bolthoff Manufacturing Co. (now Hendrie & Bolthoff Co.).

In the meantime, the McFarlane brothers, Peter and William, had come out to Central City in 1867 from Prince Edward Island, Canada. They became contractors, organizing the firm of McFarlane & Co., and were active in the rebuilding of Central City after the fire. Eventually they bought the Silas Bertenshaw shops in Black Hawk, and in 1903, the James W. Jackson shops at 15th and Wewatta in Denver, but only after purchasing the foundry in Central City from Hendrie & Bolthoff in 1882. (Frank Hall gives this date which is in variance with other dates shown for this sale.)

In 1906, the firm was reorganized into Peter McFarlane and Sons Iron Works Co., with Peter McFarlane at the head, in Central City, and the McFarlane Manufacturing Co., under William McFarlane, in Denver. Peter McFarlane, who died in May, 1929, held a mortgage on the opera house. The *Weekly Register-Call* reported on June 11, 1937, that the foundry on Eureka Street was being repaired under the direction of Frederick McFarlane, son of Peter McFarlane.

## 69. City Brewery, Boarding House and Saloon

You can't see much, but you can see portions of the old building foundations still standing across the street from the Court House.

William Lehmkuhl, an old-country brewer, set up a brewery on this site in 1866, and it prospered. In 1874, when other businesses were temporarily reduced to ashes, Lehmkuhl, far removed from the fire, did a $12,000 business with a $5,000 stock. (When you come right down to it, neither of these figures was very large when compared to the volume done that year by grocery stores, markets, and others who were burned out and had to seek temporary quarters.)

On November 15, 1877, Lehmkuhl completed the frame Eureka House adjoining his brewery. Now he combined a boarding house with brewery and saloon. (Henry Goetze had set up his Casino at Lehmkuhl's in July, 1874.) "WILLIAM LEHMKUKL Board Day & Week (Hotels, families, bars supplied with beer on short notice)," his advertisement stated.

Dan Fuelscher, Lehmkuhl's son-in-law, bought the establishment March 27, 1897, "fixing up the brewery building, making 12 new rooms which,

69

in connection with the Eureka House, will be run as a first class hotel by Mrs. Meyer after May 1." The Eureka House burned down about 1904.

## 70. Mathews Law Office

This building at one time was used as a Chinese laundry, and in other years as the low office of W. C. Mathews. It is believed to have been built around 1870, and presently serves as quarters for the Opera House cast.

## 71. Rachofsky Residence

For many years this was the home of the Rackofsky family, although not built by them. A. Rachofsky left his native Poland as a youth and arrived in New York the day Lincoln was assassinated. He came to Central City and founded the New York store, later establishing branches in Loveland and Burlington, Colorado. Upon the celebration of the Rachofsky's fiftieth wedding anniversary in 1930, it was pointed out then that Rachofsky had been in business longer than any other merchant in the state.

On August 6, 1909, is was reported that "the stone building east of the Eureka Hotel on Eureka Street is being fitted as offices of the Topeka, Frontenac and Aduddell mines." Henry P. Lowe managed these very productive mining operations, and it is thought that he may have also

**59   58**
**72**
**71**                                                **70**

lived here as well as having a mine office in this building. At present the building is used for members of the cast at the Opera House.

## 72. The Opera House

The Central City Opera House opened on the nights of March 4 and 5, 1878. It was described as the "finest temple of the Muse west of the Missouri." In 1887, a number of Central City and Black Hawk residents, determined to have an opera house "unsurpassed in Colorado," had subscribed $12,000 for its construction.

The fire of 1874 destroyed the Montana Theater. The Belvidere Theater (Armory Hall) built in 1875 to take the place of the Montana, was deemed inadequate after the Amateur Dramatic Company's performance of *The Bohemian Girl* played to overflowing audiences in the spring of 1877.

"Central is nothing if not musical," wrote Frank C. Young,* "the colony's musical talent was fairly distributed in the early days . . . various church choirs . . . The first necessity of production is a suitable theater; and since the great fire has disposed of the old Montana which

*Frank C. Young, *Echoes from Arcadia*, 1903.

72

at least had a roomy stage, with scenery, curtains and furniture, such as it was, the only place available now is the Belvidere theater . . . and this means limited space for the audience and a large amount of tinkering of one kind or another for the stage. Production of *The Bohemian Girl*, besides providing us with some weeks of interesting amusement in its preparation, proves of much more lasting and needed benefit, not only in suggesting the need of an opera house but in supplying the necessary enthusiasm to launch the project. . . ."

The Gilpin County Opera Association was formed in 1877, capitalized for $50,000, and directors elected. The board consisted of Henry M. Wolcott, William Fullerton, Dr. William Edmundson, Thomas I. Richman, and Ben Wisebart.

Frank Young continued: ". . . a company is formed and the stock subscribed to generally through the town; the desired site is secured, and plans are drawn; within a few weeks a handsome stone and brick structure is under way, and early in the next spring the new opera house is opened in a blaze of glory."

The association accepted the plans submitted by Robert S. Roeschlaub, Denver architect, native of Bavaria who served with the 84th Illinois Volunteers, and designer of many well-known buildings in Colorado.

Ground was broken for the opera house June 14, 1877. Thomas Mullen and McFarlane Brothers had the building contract; the former for the masonry, the latter, the carpentry. Amid the jubilation, there was a lament over the necessary removal of an old landmark to make way for the new building. The stage barn built in 1860 and used by Tom Pollack for a livery was moved to a new location at Baldwin's stables above Lehmkuhl's on Eureka Street.

Plans called for a structure built of Gilpin County granite, except for the top and sides. Fire walls were to be of brick. The building measured 55 by 110 feet, and the stage, 43 by 52 feet. The lower floor was designed for a seating capacity of 500; the balcony, 250 persons. The dress circle and parquet were fitted with patent opera chairs. Frescoes, wall panels, a drop curtain, and a chandelier with 100 gas jets completed the setting.

The frescos and scenic work were done by J. C. Massman, a San Franciscan who had already "won a reputation in connection with the Presbyterian Church in Denver." Furnace, hot air pipes, and heating apparatus were installed by Bacon & Sons of Denver—"the building is very comfortable . . . works like a charm."

Frank Young continued: "It was built in 1878 by a lavishly generous popular subscription. Not a gesture of vain-glory, but because a whole

community loved good music and fine drama and wanted it fittingly
housed—only the best could satisfy the 'Little Kingdom of Gilpin'—only
the best of everything. . . It was at first supposed that $12,000 would do
it but an additional $6,000 had to be paid by the stockholders, so event-
ually the entire building cost between $20,000 and $25,000."

The Amateur Dramatic Company laid plans well for the opening nights,
March 1 and 3, 1878. Both opening performances were sell-outs. Special
trains began unloading visitors from Denver, Boulder, Idaho Springs, and
other mountain and plains towns several days before the premiere. The
Amateurs selected plain fare to initiate the new Opera House: musical
offerings, with the faithful participating, the first night; a drama, "School,"
and a farce, "Cool as a Cucumber," the next evening, both staged by the
Amateurs and liberally sprinkled with solos and duets.

Thereafter, such notables of the theater as Edwin Booth, Lotta Crabtree,
Emma Abbott, Mme. Janauschek, and many others, in addition to amateur
productions, played the Opera House. But dark days were ahead.

As mining, the peg on which Gilpin County economy was hung, began
a decline, only faintly discernible though it was at first, so did support
of the theater. The old guard started the migration to Denver: The Frank
C. Youngs began it in 1880. "This year of 1880," he wrote, "which I have
set as the closing one of the 15 that are here assumed as constituting the
'golden age' of the mountain colony . . . it must be apparent that the
process of disintegration is under way." The Joseph Thatchers followed
in 1882, the George Randolphs in 1883, the James Belfords in 1885, and
the John Bests in 1887, and so on. . . .

The newspaper, in October of 1879, tells that Jack Langrishe's troupe
played in the Opera House that month, which occasion must have been
pure gall to the faithful.

Henry R. Wolcott, a trustee of the Opera Association, on November 25,
1881, proposed that the Opera House be sold to the county for a courthouse. The following month he got down to brass tacks and offered the
building to the county commissioners for $8,000. This would indicate that
the glamor and excitement of having the finest opera house in the state
had worn off, leaving a residue of financial problems.

The commissioners didn't jump at the offer, and after the palace guard
drifted away the Opera House was used for entertainment of lesser in-
tellectual substance. The Amateur Company had broken up, and while the
building was in jeopardy its use was continued for wrestling matches,
minstral shows, amateurs performances, funerals, political rallies, gradu-
ation exercises, and even motion pictures, a few decades later. The Opera

House first fell from grace, for example, on March 11, 1881, when a wrestling match was held on the stage.

In April of 1885, Buffalo Bill's company played the Opera House in "that sensational drama, The Prairie Wolf." On July 8, 1910, a No. 5 Powers cameograph was installed with the announcement that movies and illustrated songs would be shown thereafter. The machine was replaced in June, 1916, with a Powers No. 6 which was guaranteed to "eliminate shakiness." D. W. Griffith's *Birth of a Nation* was shown in 1915; *Quo Vadis,* in 1916. Then there came a time when the Opera House was closed until the renaissance of 1932.

With the restoration of the Opera House and beginning of the Festival, Lillian Gish and Raymond Hackett opened in *Camille* on July 16, 1932, amid the color and splendor of the old days. (Camille was first presented in Central City on May 17, 1872, by Jack Langrishe's company at the old Montana.) Each year since 1932—war years excepted—stars of opera, stage, and screen have played to capacity audiences in the old Opera House.

To more than anything else, the restoration was due to the foresight and faith of two women, Anne Evans and Ida Kruse McFarlane, who, as far back as 1929, envisioned the restored opera and festival. (This story is covered in detail by Caroline Bancroft in her book *Gulch of Gold.*) The Opera House was a gift to the Central City Opera House Association through the University of Denver by heirs of Peter McFarlane, builder of the Opera House: Fred and George McFarlane, and their sister, Mrs. Yetta McFarlane Schroder.

Frank Hitchens, for many years master of properties at the Opera House, died September, 1940, in Denver. William (Billy) Hamilton, custodian and keeper of the keys for many years, died in the fall of 1960. Billy laid the marble-floor entrance to the Opera House in 1940. The stairway was built from court to balcony in the same year, and in August, the walk between the buildings was replaced by a new one.

The arrastre in the yard is typical of the first such crude device built in Gregory Gulch in July 1859, before the advent of slightly more efficient methods of grinding ores. It functions on the mortar and pestle principle; in this case the pestle, a large, rounded rock, is rotated inside the mortar by a horse traveling around a full circle. The ore in the mortar is thus finely ground.

In the years between 1920 and 1929, a local company, the Central City Dramatic Society, under the aegis of Rae Laird, staged amateur theatricals in the Opera House.

In summary: The Gilpin County Opera Association built the Opera House in 1877-1878; the Central City Opera House Association took shape at the beginning of the latter-day revival. For details see Caroline Bancroft's *Gulch of Gold*, Sage Books, Denver, 1958.

## 73. The Academy Reservoir

The low-roof structure near the Ida Kruse McFarlane Memorial on the slope of Gunnell Hill is known as the Academy reservoir (for St. Aloysisus Academy which once stood on the site of the memorial). It is a part of Central City's water supply system, an adjunct of the reservoir on upper Eureka Street. It also serves as a pressure reducer for the system.

## 74. The Ida Kruse McFarlane Memorial

Up on Gunnell Hill, St. Aloysisus Academy, boarding and day school, was opened January 2, 1875 under the supervision of Rev. Burion of the Sisters of St. Aloysisus.

In July of the previous year, shortly after the fire, the contract was let and ground broken on July 27, for a brick building, two and one-half stories high, 53 feet square. It was to be ready for the opening of school on September 20 that year and would accommodate 175 pupils and 35 boarders.

75              74                    73

The building was finished and topped with a cross. In 1879, a series of wooden steps were built from Pine Street up to the school building. Fr. Howlett was credited with the idea.

The school graduated many students during the years, but was torn down in the mid-1930's. The cross and foundation were retained as a memorial to Ida Kruse McFarlane, member of a pioneer Central City family, one-time head of the Department of English at Denver University, and one of the prime movers in the Opera House restoration and festival. Billy Hamilton directed construction of the memorial.

## 75. Coeur d'Alene Mine

As a mine with a production record, not much can be said for this museum piece, included herewith because of the prominent spot it occupies on the side of Gunnell Hill, and the attention it naturally attracts.

Some years ago the property was deeded to the opera association by Mrs. Effie Jenks. One of the last references to the Coeur d'Alene was a 1910 item in the *Weekly Register-Call* telling of plans to deepen the shaft from 675 to 800 feet. Apparently a depth of only 700 feet was reached. The building makes a good landmark; perhaps with the new coat of paint it receives regularly it is a symbol of the hopes people still have that mining will someday come into its own again.

## 76. Buell Mine Power Plant

This masonry shell is all that remains of the power plant used by the Buell mining operations in Gregory Gulch. Years ago, each mine had

**76**

its own steam boiler, and generators if electricity was used. This building was dismantled about 1923. The Buell mine shaft and mill were on the other side of Gregory Street which was spanned by an overpass connecting the surface buildings across the road.

The Buell was one of Gilpin County's largest producers. By 1876, over $1 million worth of minerals had been taken out; it's mill was considered the best in the region in 1874.

In 1901, the surface plant was completely rebuilt. The old mill was dismantled and replaced with one of larger capacity, and a new power plant erected. The Central City paper of February 8, 1901 reported that "on the Buell property masons are busy putting up a stone building 54 by 100 feet which is to be occupied by the engine, boilers, dynamos and coal bins."

The rise and fall of the gold mining industry in the region can pretty well be traced time-wise and county-wide by evolution and disintegration of the surface structures at the Buell.

## 77. Masonic Monument

Inscribed—"Monument to the first Masonic on this site, June 12, 1959. Preemption of one block from Gregory Mining District by William M. Slaughter, John Hughs and Joseph Casto. Dedicated by Grand Lodge Ancient and Accepted Order of Masons 1932."

Beyond is the head-frame, or gallows-frame, over the Bates Hunter Mine shaft, with the ubiquitous TV aerial, about the only thing head-frames are good for nowadays, roosting on top.

While on the subject, Bates Hunter, sometimes known as the Bates-Hunter, is the southeastern extension of the famous Bates vein as it ascends Mammoth hill. As this is now getting into the province of mining terms, it is sufficient to say that the Bates is one of the main veins or lodes of the county. Perhaps it would be truer to say that it *was* one of the main veins because it is now largely mined out, except at great depths. While the vein was discovered by John H. Gregory in 1859, it was named for Capt. William H. Bates who recorded the claim as his own, and then deeded one-half of the two hundred feet, which the law then allowed the discoverer, to Gregory.

## 78. Kruse Grocery Store

Here is another case where a building does not have a specific name. In most cases, it's easy to use the builder's surname, and were this done here the little "brick" might be called the Belden building. In any event,

78

Belden & Company established a grocery store here at Gregory Point in the 1860's—it was probably D. D. Belden, one of the early settlers. Later, in the 1880's, the store was kept by Fredrick Kruse, member of the pioneer Kruse family, who became very prominent in business and civic affairs of the county.

The little "brick" and the large, white house across the road are part and parcel and are bought and sold together. It was while living in the house that Fredrick Kruse was fatally injured in 1910 while making some repairs on the flume in front of the house.

The next owner of the frame house and brick building had the latter altered so it could be used as a garage. The building has not always stood alone. In the early days, the gulch behind it was lined with dwellings and mine structures. Well, for that matter, so was Gregory Gulch over its entire length.

Across the road, the Becker-Bates shaft house, still has operating machinery intact. The mine was opened in the 1860's.

## 79. Gregory Diggings

For those not wishing to leave their cars, the inscription on the monument is reproduced:

77                                    79

On This Ground Later Known As
GREGORY DIGGINGS
John H. Gregory of Georgia
Discovered the First Gold Lode
in Colorado on May 6, 1859
This Discovery Inaugurated The
Permanent Development of Colorado
The District Has Produced
$65,000,000 in Gold
Erected By
THE STATE HISTORICAL SOCIETY OF COLORADO
AND BY
THE MRS. J. N. HALL FOUNDATION
AND BY
STATE CIVIL SERVICE EMPLOYEES OF COLORADO
1932

This is good—as far as it goes—but more can be said about this historic spot. Here, at Gregory Point, a miners' meeting was held on May 8, 1859; rough mining rules were adopted which remained in effect until enactment of the Federal Mining Act of 1872. At their meeting, the miners passed resolutions that limited lode claims to 100 by 50 feet and placer, or "creek," claims to 100 feet along the gulch. (Lode and vein mean the same thing.) At later meetings on July 9 and 16, 1859, a local provisional government was organized.

80

## 80. The Gaston Mine

Putting it another way, this wooden building on the skyline represents a gold mine; its obvious idleness and solitary appearance symbolize the plight of the gold mining industry in Gilpin County, in Colorado, and in all the gold-producing states of the nation. What, mined out? Oh, no. Plenty of the stuff left but it can't be mined. Why? Well, ask somebody who knows.

Actually, besides an image, you see a shaft house over the shaft of the Gaston mine. The Gaston on rich Bates hill was discovered in 1859 by James Gaston. By 1871, it was in the possession of Louis P. Arrighi, and ten years later A. L. Whittaker and J. Washburn of Denver were developing the Gaston, "close by the Bobtail, Gregory and Bates." Fossett reported that there was very rich ore near the surface but, strangely enough, the shaft in 1881 was only 70 feet deep. The present shaft house was built in 1923 and the shaft is now 300 feet deep.

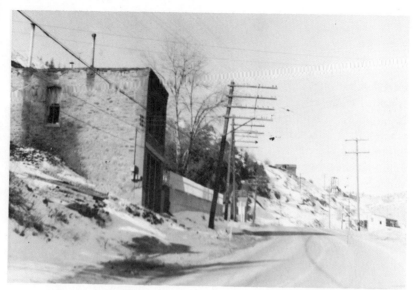

81

## 81. Masonry House

Here is another building without a name. It is worthy of attention because, according to the present owner, it dates back to the early 1860's. He believes there was a carriage shop on the ground floor in the early days, but within the memory of man the upstairs has always been used for living quarters. Old photos show that the building was once surrounded by dwellings and mine buildings.

# BLACK HAWK

Black Hawk is the lowermost town in a series of communities that once extended the length of Gregory Gulch and beyond. Beginning with Black Hawk, at the junction of Gregory Gulch and North Clear Creek, there were Mountain City, Central City, and on up Nevada Gulch, Nevada or Nevadaville or Bald Mountain.

The name Black Hawk was derived through a chain of events. A quartz mill, manufactured by the Black Hawk Company in Rock Island, Illinois, and named after the famous Indian chief, was delivered to Messrs. Lee, Judd and Lee at the present site of Black Hawk on May 5, 1860. Alonzo Smith, a company mechanic, left Rock Island with the mill on February 22, 1860, arriving at the mill site on North Clear Creek two and one-half months later. The trip had been attended by many hardships, one of which was crossing the Missouri River on ice floes.

The Black Hawk mill, the first in the new gold country, was set up and put into operation at a site later occupied by the Fifty Gold Mines mill (behind the motel). The same year the townsite was laid out, and a post office established at what was then known as Black Hawk Point, Gilpin County, Colorado Territory, on December 6, 1862. On February 8, 1871, the name was changed to Black Hawk, and then to Blackhawk on January 30, 1895, and again to Black Hawk July 1, 1950.

Black Hawk became an incorporated city by act of the territorial legislature approved March 11, 1864. (Central City was incorporated at the same time.) In 1900, the population was over 1200 but in 1960 it had fallen to 171. In the early days, everyone was dependent, directly or indirectly, upon the mining industry. Today, many of the residents commute daily to jobs in Golden and Denver.

A narrow-gauge line of the Colorado Central Rrailroad, building up Clear Creek Canon from Golden, reached Black Hawk in 1872. It was extended to Central City over the switchback or highline in 1878. Crude smelting ore and mineral concentrates were shipped out to the valley points from Black Hawk, the principal railhead in the county. Concentrating mills were located here because water was available from North Clear Creek, more than elsewhere. An old mill building with the ends knocked out served as the first depot. Track was laid through the center and whatever advantage was gained in shelter was lost in smoke and cinders.

Through the years, probably Black Hawk's most pressing civic problems have had to do with water: water for drinking and water that floods Gregory Gulch and the streets during summer cloudbursts. It overflows the streets with sand, mud, and debris. With the problem of the flume goes the problem of the boardwalk that covers it. After the fire in 1874, a walk of sorts was built to connect Black Hawk and Central City. Only a year later it began to give trouble and has continued to do so ever since. Witness a notice printed in the Central City paper March 2, 1875: "We have been requested by several parties to call attention of the proper authorities to the condition of the plank walk over the flume through Black Hawk. The holes are becoming too numerous for comfort." That was in 1875 and it has been a constant struggle between man and nature ever since to keep this line of communication open between the two towns.

The railroad between Black Hawk and Central City was pulled out in the 1920's. The last scheduled train left Black Hawk for Denver on May 4, 1941, just before that portion was dismantled also.

Black Hawk was never ravished by fire the way Central City, Cripple Creek, and other mining camps were, and then rebuilt. A few of Black Hawk's commercial buildings, still standing, were erected in the 1860's.

Electric locomotive and ore train leaving Bobtail tunnel, about 1900, en route to mill in Black Hawk. Note high trolley pole and wire used to clear road. *Denver Public Library Western Collection.*

Clean-up in Black Hawk after one especially bad flood left streets covered with mud. Railroad company built temporary track to load out cars with debris which was dumped downstream. Note Gilpin Hotel on right and railroad highline to Central City in the background. *Winifred Fritz Collection.*

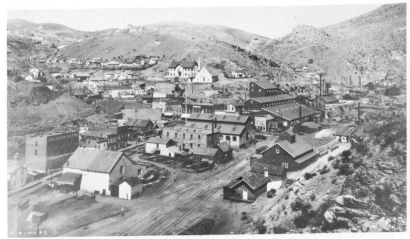

Black Hawk, once the city of ore processing mills and smelters, as it appeared when gold mining was supreme. Ore treatment works extended along Clear Creek beyond borders of picture, which was probably taken about 1900. Now, only the school, the hotel, several churches, and a few other buildings remain; the railroad, and the smoke and noise of industry are gone. *Denver Public Library Western Collection.*

Black Hawk about 1905, looking up Gregory Gulch toward Central City. Narrow-gauge train with Colorado and Southern engine No. 12 has just crossed bridge after descending switchback from Central City. *Louella Fritz collection.*

82

# 82. Placer Mining

A few words about gold panning, or placer mining, or the what-are-those-people-doing-down-along-the-creek aspect of Gilpin County tourism. By definition, a placer is a place where gold particles may be recovered by washing and separating the alluvial or glacial deposits in a stream bed. (This definition assumes, of course, that gold is there in the first place, that the stream is in a gold mining region.) Placer gold—flakes, grains, or nuggets—being heavy is carried down into stream beds after eroding from gold vein outcrops, or "mother lodes."

In the years—now over 100—since gold was first discovered in Clear Creek and its branches and tributaries, the "ground" has been dug and worked over many times. The unsightly piles of rock were left by dredges, but every foot of creek bottom has probably been turned over by men with pick and shovel and gold pan, rocker, cradle, or sluice. All placering methods, whether by hand shovel, power shovel, or dredge, depend upon two physical properties of gold: First, being heavier than rock, gold settles to the bottom when agitated in a mixture of sand, rock, mud, and water and is separated by washing away the debris. Next, gold and mercury are attracted to each other and by this principle gold is trapped by the mercury. The resulting mixture, called amalgam, is heated in a still. This leaves a gold residue or retort. The vaporized mercury is condensed and reused.

Several parties working on North Clear Creek have power shovels and mechanical equipment for placer mining. Others are panning gold for the thrills that have always accompanied the search for the yellow metal. It's possible to get a string of "color" in the pan but it's slow, back-breaking work if pursued seriously. In the depression days of the 1930's, the banks of Clear Creek were lined with people eking out a few dollars a day— enough to buy beans and keep off the dole.

Finally, to the inevitable question: If the gold is there why isn't it being mined. The answer is simple. At a fixed price of only $35 an ounce, it takes a lot of gold to pay the high cost of labor, equipment, and supplies and make a profit. And there just isn't that much gold.

# 83. The Presbyterian Church

The Presbyterian Church and the Black Hawk school house are almost inseparable landmarks on the side of Bates Hill overlooking Black Hawk.

Of the two buildings, the church is the older. It was organized February 15, 1863 by the Rev. George W. Warner, and the building dedicated in

106

|       |       |      | 84   |      | 83   |
|-------|-------|------|------|------|------|
| 96    | 95    |      | 94   |      |      |

August 1863. The bell in the belfy was the first in any Presbyterian church west of the Mississippi River and was brought across the plains by ox-cart. Electric lights were installed in the building September 17, 1897.

But as mining declined, so did the population, and in October of 1907 the First Presbyterian Church of Black Hawk issued a warranty deed for the building and lots 13 and 14 to Black Hawk school district No. 3 for a consideration of $600. Thereafter the church building was used as the school gymnasium.

## 84. The Black Hawk Schoolhouse

The school on the hill opened for classes April 30, 1870; the last class used the building in May 1960. School consolidation went into affect in 1960, and since then all Black Hawk students attend grade and high school in Central City. But during the 90 years the Black Hawk school was in use one Black Hawk family, the Blakes, was represented by one or more members attending during the entire time classes were held in this building.

School district No. 3 was organized in Black Hawk November 7, 1863 in the law offices of Reimine & Marsh. Chalk up some firsts for the county schools. The first permanent schoolhouses in Colorado were built in Gilpin County; the stone building in Central City at a cost of $20,000; the frame building in Black Hawk for $15,000. (Costs seem high because material and supplies were freighted in by team before the railroad era.)

The two buildings on the hill appear in historical photos which portray Black Hawk and Gregory Gulch as one of the most active mining camps in Colorado. But there were some people who thought it was not a pretty sight. For instance, Bayard Taylor, writing of his visit in 1866, described the Presbyterian Church as "the sole pleasant object . . . above the chimneys and ravines." Before school opened in the fall of 1878, steps were built from Selak Street to Church Street "for a short cut to school."

## 85. The Lace House

The Lace House, it is believed, was built and occupied in the 1860's by a family named Osborne. Details are lacking. Later, in the 1890's, the Pirchers lived here. Man and boy, this was home to Lou Pircher, Gilpin Tramway superintendent from 1904 to 1913.

85

Lou left Black Hawk to work for the Moffat Road at Tabernash, later going with the Union Pacific in Denver. Lou recalls the Tramway years, and the nights he would lie awake waiting for the whistle as the train passed the Freedom mine, the signal that all was well.

As time went on, the city of Black Hawk assumed ownership of the Lace House, renting it to various tenants until it was sold in 1920 for $20! One stipulation of the sale required that the house be painted and kept in good condition and repair at all times. The roof has been replaced, but other than that nothing much has been done. *Sunday Empire* magazine says that house is one of the few remaining examples of rococo architecture.

Lou Pircher tried for many years to regain ownership. Others have attempted unsuccessfully to buy the Lace House, but it doesn't seem to be on the market.

## 86. The Gilpin Hotel

The first Gilpin Hotel—a frame affair built in the late 60's—is now the kitchen of the present hotel. About 1896, Julius Kline moved the old building back from the street and built the new hotel around it.

After the Colorado House burned down, Mrs. Kit Murphey took over the Gilpin and ran it until about 1911. Then the O'Toole family of hotel fame assumed management and operated it until around 1915. Then a Mrs. Jungman ran the hotel until 1916 when it was sold to Joe Borzago for $500 and managed by Mrs. Hazel Manual until 1924, and then by Mrs. Anna Nelson up until about 1927. It was bought about then by Otto and Ruth Blake, and another succession of owners and operators followed.

86                                        84      83
                                          91

One of the many floods that cascaded down Gregory Gulch caused unusually bad damage to Black Hawk in 1910. It filled the street in front of the hotel with several feet of mud, sand, silt, and debris. Since it was before the days of portable earth-moving equipment, the problem was solved when the railroad built a temporary track up the street. The unwelcome dirt was loaded on flat cars and hauled down stream and dumped. After 261 cars were loaded out, the newspaper estimated that the job was at the half-way point.

Many hotels, inns and dead-falls have come and gone in Black Hawk and Central City, but the Gilpin, along with the Teller House, has purveyed food, shelter and drink for almost 100 years.

## 87. The Polar Star Mill

This is the remains of an ore stamp mill built in the 1860's. Today it is a storehouse; its contents would excite the fancy of any antique collector.

Behind and to the right of the mill building, ore was transferred from hopper-bottom cars of the two-foot Gilpin Tram, which were run up on a trestle, into the three-foot, narrow-guage cars of the Colorado and Southern, and its predecessors. From here, the ore was shipped to smelters in Golden, Denver, Leadville and Pueblo. The three-foot track had a third rail to accommodate the two-foot tram cars operating within the town limits of Black Hawk.

At this site in 1906, several hundred delegates to the Democratic National Convention in Denver were transferred from Colorado and Southern

87

cars to makeshift observation cars on the tram for a sightseeing and picnic trip to upper Gilpin County.

To entertain Colorado Editorial Association delegates in May 1911, someone proposed to take them on an "unparalleled trip" in the mountains. The delegates would ride ??00 feet into the Newhouse Tunnel at Idaho Springs. Upon reaching the Old Town mine shaft, they would be hoisted to the surface and entrain aboard Gilpin Tram cars for the trip down to the Polar Star mill in Black Hawk, and then return to Idaho Springs on the Colorado and Southern train. Probably nothing ever came of the scheme, which had interesting possibilities, but the story serves to tell of at least one destination reached by the Newhouse Tunnel under Gilpin County.

The old mill at the left of the Polar Star was the Empire. On the hill beyond, the large white house was once owned and occupied by Nathaniel P. Hill, a one-time senator from Colorado. Hill was probably best known for perfecting a smelting process to treat Gilpin County ores.

## 88. Knights of Pythias Building

The present ground floor of this building, built about 1864, was originally the second floor. Floods washing down Gregory Gulch have deposited silt and debris around the original first floor which is now the basement. Early photos show a stairway leading up to the present ground-level floor.

Floods have plagued Black Hawk—and Central City, too, for that matter—since the beginning.

The Knights of Pythias lodge hall was upstairs, Jesse Scobey's saloon,

88

below. After Scobey, the place was leased to George Snyder. Others followed and for almost one hundred years, prohibition days excepted, it has been used as a bar and billiard establishment. Before the city hall was built, the town council met in the Knights of Pythias lodge rooms.

Below this building a frame store housed the Colorado Shop, a shoe store and repair shop operated by William A. Douglas, founder of the shoe store chain of that name. On the other side, two frame buildings were used respectively by a wholesale and retail grocery and dry goods house, and a wholesale meat company.

Behind the motel and K. of P. building the Fifty Gold Mines mill operated for many years until dismantled a number of years ago. For many years gold ore was brought by electric mine train from the Bobtail tunnel, through another tunnel in Bates Hill opposite the Bobtail, to a point on the hillside above the mill. The rock retaining wall that carried the track between tunnel portal and mill is still in place and easily seen from the highway. The narrow-gauge railroad grade is also recognizable nearby as it climbs up to the switchback and on to Central City.

## 89. The Boiler Works

The large stone building at the foot of Gregory Gulch near the highway junction was erected by George Stroehle, a pioneer boiler maker of the region. At one time, the business was known as the Black Hawk Boiler and Sheet Iron Works. Nowadays, the building is used as a county highway maintenance garage.

George Stoehle came to Black Hawk in 1864. He was raised in a border town between Germany and Austria, and migrated to the United States in 1852, settling in Rock Island, Illinois, where he learned the boiler-making trade. He enlisted in the 45th Illinois Regiment when the Civil War began, but came to Gilpin County after being mustered out of the Union army. Here his services were in great demand because the mines were steam-powered.

That same year he returned to Illinois for his family, bringing them out by wagon. While crossing Cherry Creek in Denver, his outfit was nearly lost in the quicksand. Legend has it that he traded his mules for a house in Central City used by the Chinese for a laundry. It was in this building the fire started in 1874 that destroyed Central City.

Lathes, planers, shapers, drills, and other machines, many freighted across county by ox team, are still in use in the boiler works buildings.

George Stroehle died in 1911 and his son, John, operated the business until a few years ago.

112

89     90     92

## 90. Fick's Carriage Shop

Under the Bull Durham sign the village smitty stood, shoeing horses and making quality carriages and ore wagons.

In May of 1879, Matt Boellert built this wagon shop in Black Hawk. The partnership of Leitbman & Boellert, formed in November of that year, became Fick & Boellert in 1880. Fick went on alone in the shop until 1906 when the business was purchased by Thorvold Crook. He promptly sold or leased to Shea & Ryan who disposed of the business the following year to A. Beck.

Beck ran it until about 1911, after which it was idle until Fred Bouchette took over sometime between 1915 and 1917. As a wagon and carriage shop, the last stand against the automobile was made by A. Blood who stuck it out another year or two. Then the building was used as a garage and storage place owned by Joe Heppberger until some placer miners purchased it in 1954.

The frame building next to Fick's is the old Heppberger home where four sons and two daughters were raised by the Heppbergers. Engle Heppberger and his sons were in the teamster business, hauling ore down from the mines. The building is still owned by a member of the family.

113

86                         91

## 91. Ben Olson's

This building housed Ben Olson's "Cabinet" until his demise in 1923.
It was originally owned by Scandia Lodge I.O.O.F No. 6 until consolidation with No. 3 about 1912. The former, as the name implies, was com-
prised of Scandanavians, while the latter, meeting around the corner, had
a membership that was largely "Cousin Jack."

In later years, several antique shops have had a try at this spot. The
upstairs apartments, however, never want for tenants. The little frame
house next door housed a bakery about 1904, but for many years it has
also been used for living quarters.

## 92. The Railroad Switchback

Leaving Black Hawk on highway 119 toward Denver, long scars are
noticeable on the mountainside to the right. This is an old railroad
grade and all that's left of the switchback or highline between Black
Hawk and Central City, built in 1878.

In 1872, the narrow-gauge line of the Colorado Central Railroad reached
Black Hawk from Golden. At the Forks (where U. S. 6 and Colorado 119
split now) another branch of the railroad built toward Idaho Springs and

92

Georgetown. The panic of 1873 halted extension of the line from Black Hawk to Central City and travelers were obliged to use horse-drawn conveyances in order to reach Central City from Black Hawk until May 21, 1878, when the four-mile switchback was completed at a cost of $65,000.

Since it was obviously impossible to build the railroad straight up Gregory Gulch to Central City, a switchback was required. This enabled the roadbed to climb in stages, rising 540 feet in four miles. A long bridge carried the track over Gregory Gulch at a point near the Black Hawk city hall. The switchback iron was taken up in 1925, and the rest of the line from Black Hawk to Golden, in 1941. Now the old grade makes an excellent foot or bridle path, with a magnificent view to go with the exercise.

The switchback is worthy of more than just passing mention, and would probably go unnoticed by all save the railroad buffs who would take it home if they could.

## 93. The Hardware Block

This block owned and occupied by the harware company was built in 1875 by Marsh and Buffington. A newspaper item of January 1876 said that "Sheriff Buffington is one-half owner of a fine brick block in Black Hawk, has a $60,000 bank account, is good looking and dresses well. . ."

For many years Lowell & Clark operated a hardware store here until the partnership was dissolved in 1897. The upper floor had apartments and a meeting room later known as Fritz Hall. In 1901, Clark and Rogers succeeded E. E. Clark.

At one time Sam Smith's bank occupied one of the store rooms; Eugene F. Ballard was cashier in April of 1881. Back in December 1875, George Brubaker "moved his entire stock of groceries into the new store of Marsh & Buffington."

A beserk itinerant, living with his family in one of the apartments, in 1900 killed his 17-year old daughter, fatally wounded his wife, and then attempted suicide. A lynching was averted when the killer was moved to Denver and lodged in the county hospital.

Earlier, Ottoback & Co. ran the Western meat market here. On the site a drug store and the United States post office was operated by Harper Orahood & Nesmith.

The hardware store business has been conducted by the present owners since 1922. Before that it was, in reverse order, Clark Hardware, Clark & Rogers, Eugene Clark, Lowell & Clark, Wells & Lowell, B. F. Wells, and the first operator, Frank Lowell.

The store's first gasoline pump, installed in September 1916, was a refueling point for early-day motorists traveling from the valley to the tungsten boom town of Nederland. The newspaper hailed the installation

84        83
94        93

116

as a great improvement over the practice of dispensing gasoline from small containers.

## 94. Golden Beer

Here is another late 1860 block built of sand brick made in Central City. It was erected by I.O.O.F. Lodge No. 3, the Cousin Jacks who later consolidated with the Scandanavians in Lodge No. 6 around the corner.

Within this century, the up-hill store room was occupied by A. Lipp's meat market, the lower (next to the hardware store), by J. C. Martin's drug store. After the drug store it became a saloon where Golden beer was drawn.

In later years, the entire upstairs was used as a meeting hall by the Rebekahs until around 1915. Since then all parts of the building have been used as a storehouse.

## 95. Richards Building

## 96. Sullivan Building

The upper of these two almost identical buildings was erected in the early 1870's; the lower, a few years later. Comparing certain features of

100   99     98      96    95            94

the two, it is evident that both are of the same design and construction and were probably put up by one owner or builder. The most obvious though minor difference is the size and shape of the lower window casings, and the slight variance in ground floor elevations.

The names used are those of later tenants, not of the original occupants. The upper structure was erected about the same year as the school, in 1870. For many years Mike Sullivan ran a saloon here, and a Dr. Lynn had offices and living quarters upstairs. At the rear, on Salak Street, a sign on the door still reads "FREE AND HOT LUNCHES BETWEEN 10 A.M. AND 2 P.M."

The lower building first began to appear in Black Hawk scenes of the later 1870's. Jim Richards conducted a grocery and variety store on the ground floor and used the upstairs for lodging. Later the entire first floor of the two buildings was joined to make a dance hall. There have been no occupants for a number of years.

## 97. Black Hawk City Hall

The city hall, completed December 6, 1877 at a cost of $5,000, stands on the site of Black Hawk's first jail and Judge Haight's office. Prior to its completion, the town fathers met in the Knights of Pythias lodge rooms

97

down the street. When the new building was turned over to the town, the occasion was marked by a large banquet served on the second floor. Traditionally, the first floor has always housed fire-fighting equipment, some new, some not so new. As did all towns, Black Hawk had its share of fire but never the devastating kind that destroyed Central City, Cripple Creek and other camps.

## 98. Antique Shop Row

For nearly 100 years this row of frame buildings has survived the attack of flood, fire, and age, outlasting many brick contemporaries. Furthermore, it is believed that these frame structures actually predate some of the nearby brick buildings.

For as long as anyone can remember, all three have been fitted with upstairs living quarters. In the farthest uphill building, a Dr. Richmond had both dwelling and office space upstairs, while on the ground floor, the Rocky Mountain Inn, the town sweet shop, was in business for many years. Ice cold drinks, fountain service, ice cream, and notions were sold in the early 1900's, according to a sign over the door.

A barber shop was in the lower building for years, followed by Mrs.

100  99                          98

100   99

Bennett's restaurant. Business was so good that the dining space was expanded into the lower floor of the center building.

For the last ten years, all three buildings have been used for antique shops. Selak Street originally cut off from Gregory and ran in front of this row and the city hall. It was once a principal business street of Black Hawk, all but obliterated now.

## 99 - 100. Old Post Office Building

For many years the Black Hawk (and Blackhawk) post office was located in this building before being moved to the present quarters in 1958. From an examination of photographs, it is estimated that the structure was erected in the late 1860's or early 1870's.

Even before the post office, a bank occupied the first floor. The vault used by the postmasters is still in the building. In the early days, the upstairs was used for living quarters.

Thorvold Crook leased the second floor in 1909 to the Black Hawk tribe No. 84 I.O.R.M., and added a back room for lodge meetings. Otto Blake owned the building at one time while the post office was still here. Title is now with the V.F.W. post.

120

On the adjoining side, the Martin Miller building was fitted with living quarters upstairs, a barber shop with hot bath facilities downstairs.

The ruins of a building on the west side marks the location of C. B. Klais' dry goods and shoe store, a Black Hawk enterprise for many years.

## 101. The Corner Grocery

The Corner Grocery has always been the corner grocery in Black Hawk—since the early 1860's, in fact. While its earlier days are obscure, later years are easily traced. Robins & Sheerer bought out Sleep & Metcalf in 1896. (Some say that Black Hawk was without the services of an undertaker. One Mr. Sleep did offer professional services along that line, according to newspaper ads.)

In 1902, the store was operated as Robins & Blake, then just John L. Robin's grocery. It was purchased by Joe Borzago in 1910 and run by him until his death in 1944. Numerous storekeepers have been here since then.

## 102. The Masonic Building

The next building up-hill from the corner grocery store is the most recent masonry addition to the Black Hawk business district.

101  102  103  104  105

It was built by Black Hawk lodge No. 11, A.F.&.A.M. in 1910. (This lodge was installed February 17, 1866.) It was planned that the lower floor would be used by Joseph Borzago as a storage adjunct to his grocery store next door. Up to the time the new building was erected, the lodge had been meeting over the grocery.

Since 1958, the ground floor has been used for the Black Hawk post office, and regular lodge meetings are still held in the upper floors.

## 103. Black Hawk Mercantile Building

This is not an official name, or even a popular one for this old building, but since this name is visible on the weathered lettering in front it will serve for this purpose.

In the 1880's, a sign in the same spot proclaimed C. Miller's Cash Market, and at another time, Miller & Koch. Much later the building housed Joseph Borzago's grocery store until he bought out Robins. It was vacant from 1910 until 1946 when a door was added and converted into the county equipment maintenance shop. After that it reverted to private ownership and has been condemned as being unsafe for use.

## 104. The Rohling Building

For many years this building was owned by J. H. Phillip Rohling, German immigrant, later a merchant prince and mayor of Black Hawk. Rohling served his apprenticeship with a clothing store in Indianapolis, established one of his own in that city, and then moved the entire stock to Black Hawk in 1884.

Rohling bought and moved into what came to be known as the Rohling building which dates back to the early 1860's (builder unknown). (That the structure was built in the 60's is ascertained by study of photographs of that period.)

Rohling's store occupied the left half of the building on two floors, each 25 by 80 feet in size. In 1896, Rohling opened a shoe store on Main Street in Central City. The lettering Phillip S. Rohling is faintly discernable over the doorway of the Black Hawk building. The other side of the building also had a clothing store at one time, the establishment of S. Tobolowsky. The upstairs was divided into apartments. The Baby Doe of fact and fiction is supposed to have been a tenant here with her husband upon their arrival from Wisconsin in the 70's.

In more recent years, the entire upstairs has been used as lodging and sleeping quarters, while the downstairs was modified for dances, movies and other amusements.

Between the right side of this building and the one next west, a high bridge built in 1878 carried the narrow-gauge railroad across Gregory Street and Gulch on the first leg of the climb to Central City. The bridge was dismantled in the early 1940's.

Here are examples of three distinct building periods. The half-circle arches are typical of Central City and Black Hawk (and Denver) buildings of the 1860's; the slightly rounded ones, the 1870's. Those with the rectangular form date from the 80's and 90's to the present. These buildings were once the lower end of a solid row of brick and frame structures extending all the way to Central City.

## 105. Crook's Palace

The fifth surviving member of the string of buildings that once extended to Central City, was originally the frame, two-story Skylight saloon. Tom Crook dismantled it in 1900, and erected the present building.

## 106. Blake's Livery

Built in 1863, this livery and stable is one of the oldest commercial buildings extant in Gilpin County. Ed Blake bought out Bitzer. Blake's son, Otto, began working out of this building with the livery, drayage,

84

106

107

108

and a contracting business in 1898. Although that line of business has long since gone, Otto has operated the adjacent service station for many years.

## 107. The Black Hawk Methodist Church

This is the second Methodist church building in Black Hawk, and was erected during the pastorate of Rev. George Wallace between 1869 and 1871. The first church building was located on Swede Hill, across from the garage, but was destroyed and washed away by a flash flood in the early 1860's.

The Black Hawk church was organized in September 1892 when the congregation separated from the Central City group. It was first the Black Hawk-Arvada charge under B. T. Vincent, presiding elder of the Denver district of the Methodist Episcopal church. In later years, it was in the Black Hawk, Russell Gulch and Nevadaville circuit.

Nowadays the building is used only for Sunday School and for occasional funerals.

## 108. The Bobtail Tunnel

Bobtail Hill is cut vertically by many rich lodes, or gold-bearing veins, which were found on the surface only a short time after placer gold was discovered in the stream bed of Gregory Gulch in 1859. (Ore from one of the first workings was hauled by a bobtailed ox, thus Bobtail Hill, the Bobtail mine, and so on.)

At first these veins or lodes were mined from shafts sunk from the surface. But shafts and workings soon fill with water and must be pumped out, and ore must be hoisted to the top, and as the workings get deeper it becomes more costly to mine from shafts. Then, when and where possible, a tunnel is driven under the workings so that gravity can drain the water and help extract the ore. That was the reason for driving the Bobtail tunnel.

The Bobtail tunnel was begun in 1871 or 1872. The Fisk vein was reached (these veins are almost vertical, like the frosting in a cake that's been turned on the side) at 572 feet in 1873, the Bobtail vein at 1,100 and some feet.

A reporter of that period wrote: "A large excavation in the solid rock at the head of the tunnel [at the Bobtail vein] and 471 feet below the surface of the hill, contains huge engines and boilers for propelling the hoisting machinery and the great pumps. A brick and iron smokestack extends up the old shaft to daylight." (The pumps and hoisting equipment were for workings below the tunnel level.) Some of the old brick and iron can still be seen at the tunnel face. The tunnel was driven by hand drilling (for the blast holes) and black powder.

At first, ore cars were hauled by mule-power. In November 1881, a new electric tram line connected the Bobtail tunnel and the mill at Black Hawk. (The mill was located behind the motel site. All that can be seen of it now is the tailings dump—sand left after minerals have been extracted.) The tram track, starting inside the tunnel, ran from the portal across the then-dirt road, swung westerly and entered a now caved-in tunnel where the pine tree stands within sight of the Bobtail tunnel. The ore trains emerged at a point above the mill in Black Hawk from which the ore was dumped into bins at the mill.

After the Bobtail tram line ceased operating many years ago, ore was loaded into wagons or trucks from a now-dismantled trestle along the road.

# ACKNOWLEDGMENTS

For their assistance in providing historical data, suggesting sources of information, checking notes and manuscript for accuracy and fact, and for going along with this idea, heartfelt thanks to the following persons:

William O. Ziege, county commissioner and a native of Central City; Leroy and Mrs. Williams, prominent attorney and long-time residents; George Ramstetter, mayor and business man; Earl Quiller, one-time business man who died in early 1961; George Springer, proprietor of the long-established Pharmacy; the Vern Haynes, operators of another old business; Louis Carter, native son, former county judge, and member of the Public Utilities Commission; the Fullertons, sons of William Fullerton, early-day Gilpin County mine operator; Sid Squib, a Central City and Colorado historian; the Blakes of Black Hawk; Mona Robb of Central City; Louella Fritz of Black Hawk; George D. Harris of Denver.

Also John C. Jenkins, Jr., Central City merchant and public-spirited citizen, for providing details about origins of buildings on Lawrence Street; Don Kemp, another native son, author of the invaluable *Colorado's Little Kingdom*, for suggestions, and assistance in identifying Central City buildings; Charles Robins, Black Hawk native son, resident and traveler, and Mrs. Robins, for naming places and dates in Black Hawk's booming, and later, periods of history. Charley's knowledge of the subject is encyclopedic. Also Claude Powe, editor and publisher of the Central City *Tommy-Knawker*, for the picture of Billy Hamilton dusting the Face on the Bar Room Floor, and for valuable suggestions.

Also the ever-patient, gracious and helpful librarians of the Western History Department of the Denver Public Library and of the State Historical Society of Colorado.

Also Miss Caroline Bancroft, Gilpin County and Colorado history authority and author of many books within these subjects, for reading the manuscript, offering valuable suggestions.

Also Rae Laird, editor and publisher of the Central City *Weekly Register-Call*, for granting access to newspaper files, for reading and correcting copy fact-wise, and especially for his interest in this project; William C. Russell, Jr., adopted native son and proprietor of the Central Gold Mine and Mining and Historical Museum, authority on things historical, for painstakingly helping in making additions and corrections to the copy, and for valuable suggestions.

Finally, credit and thanks to Don Bloch, proprietor of the Collector's Centers in Central City and Denver, for suggesting this motif of Central City, "then and now," and for reading copy and offering suggestions.

Old-style type for cover, courtesy of Rae Laird of the *Weekly Register-Call.*

# SUGGESTED READING

*The Rush to the Rockies: Background of Colorado History,* James Grafton Rogers, State Historical Society of Colorado, Denver, 1957.

*Here They Dug the Gold,* George Willison, Reynal and Hitchcock, New York, 1946.

*History of the State of Colorado,* Frank Hall, Blakely, Chicago, 1889-1895.

*History of Colorado,* Wilbur F. Stone, Clarke, Chicago, 1918.

*History of Colorado,* State Historical and Natural History Society of Colorado, Denver, 1927.

*History of Clear Creek and Boulder Valleys, Colorado,* Baskin, Chicago, 1880.

*Colorado, Its Gold and Silver Mines,* Frank Fossett, Crawford, New York, 1880.

*Echoes from Peak to Plain,* Isaac N. Beardsley, Curts and Jennings, Cincinnati, 1898.

*Echoes from Arcadia,* Frank C. Young, Denver, 1903.

*Mining in Colorado,* C. W. Henderson, Government Printing Office, 1926.

*A Guide to Central City,* Caroline Bancroft, World Press, Denver, 1946.

*Colorado's Little Kingdom,* Donald C. Kemp, Sage Books, Denver, 1949.

*Denver, South Park & Pacific,* M. C. Poor, Rocky Mountain Railroad Club, Denver, 1949.

*Stampede to Timberline,* Muriel Sibell Wolle, University of Colorado, Boulder, 1949.

*Guide to the Colorado Mountains,* Colorado Mountain Club, edited by Robert M. Ormes, Sage Books, Denver, 1952.

*The Colorado Story,* LeRoy and Ann Hafen, Old West, Denver, 1953.

*Historic Central City,* Caroline Bancroft, Bancroft Pamphlets, Denver, 1957.

*Colorado's Century of Cities,* Don and Jean Griswold, Smith-Brooks, Denver, 1958.

*Gulch of Gold,* Caroline Bancroft, Sage Books, Denver, 1958.

*The Gilpin Tram,* Frank R. Hollenback, Sage Books, Denver, 1958.

*Guide to the Colorado Ghost Towns and Mining Camps,* Perry G. Eberhart, Sage Books, Denver, 1959.